SHORT NATURE WALKS

ON LONG ISLAND

Sixth Edition

by
Rodney and Priscilla Albright

revised and edited by
Robert L. Wendt

The Globe Pequot Press

Old Saybrook, Connecticut

Photography credits: Pages xii, 4, and 58, Long Island State Park Commission; page 38, Ward Melville Heritage Organization; page 92, D.E. Tripp; page 144, John Hollingsworth/Department of Interior Fish and Wildlife Service; pages 118 and 162, Robert L. Wendt

Cover photo: copyright © Jack McConnell/McConnell McNamara
Cover design: Saralyn D'Amato-Twomey
Map credits: Basic data courtesy of Lawrence G. Paul

Library of Congress Cataloging-in-Publication Data

Albright, Rodney.
    Short nature walks on Long Island / by Rodney and Priscilla
    Albright : revised and edited by Robert L. Wendt. —6th ed.
        p.   cm. — (Short nature walks series)
        ISBN 0-7627-0216-8
        1. Hiking—New York (State)—Long Island—Guidebooks.   2. Long
    Island (N.Y.)—Guidebooks.   I. Albright, Priscilla.   II. Wendt, Robert
    L.   III. Title.   IV. Series
    GV199.42.N652L662   1998   98-5453
    917.47'210443—dc21   CIP

Manufactured in the United States of America
Sixth Edition/Second Printing

To The Nature Conservancy

Contents

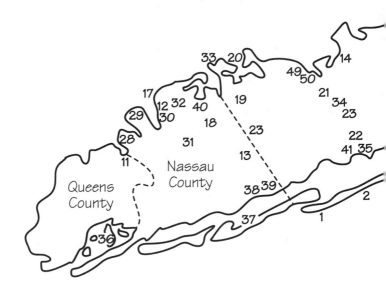

33 20

49 50 14

17 21

12 32 40 19 34

29 30 18 23

28 31 23 22

11 13 41 35

Nassau
Queens County
County 38 39 2

37 1

39

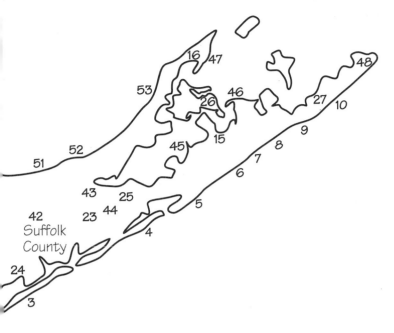

16 47
53
46
26
27 10
15
45
9
8
52 7
51 6
43 25 5
42 23 44
Suffolk
County 4
24
3
48

Map Legend

for maps accompanying walk descriptions

· — · · — ·	Preserve Boundary	▲	Viewpoint
——	Major Highway	+++++++++	Railroad
——	Other Roads	—(25)—(37)—	State and County Routes
=======	Woods Roads		
-------	Trails	★	Parking Areas
········	Choice Walks	Ⓟ	Permit Parking (see page 2)
■ ■ ■ ■ ■	Nassau–Suffolk Greenbelt Trail	W	White-Paint Blazes
· + + + + +	Long Island Greenbelt and Pine Barrens Trails	〰	Lakes and Ponds

Preface to the Sixth Edition

This edition updates the information in previous versions to reflect the constant changes that impact our island environment. Some are due to the forces of nature; others stem from population pressures and related land development. In addition, information has been added to a number of the walk descriptions and maps to enhance the reader's understanding of the local scene.

It should be no surprise that financial problems have forced public and private entities to cut staffs, close facilities, and change the hours when many parks and preserves are open. A special effort has, therefore, been made to get current schedules of hours, admission charges (if any), and telephone numbers (area code 516 unless specified) for all of the walks. Don't be surprised if there are further changes.

You should know that The Nature Conservancy, through both the Long Island chapter (250 Lawrence Hill Road, Cold Spring Harbor, NY 11724; 367–3225) and the South Fork–Shelter Island chapter (3 Railroad Avenue, P.O. Box 5125, East Hampton, NY 11937; 329–7689), manages extensive preserves here. Many are quite small, but all are unspoiled and interesting. They publish guides to them that supplement and expand admirably on the limited references to them in this volume, and give details on many others. Please respect the fact that the preserves are generally small in size and established for the protection of especially sensitive species and habitats. Considerate walkers are welcome in most of them, but it would be well to understand the nature of each and to check with the conservancy's preserve manager before venturing in.

Even though these walk descriptions are intended to attract and please casual ramblers, birders, and botanizers, we'd be remiss not to give recognition to the contributions that organized hiking groups have made to walking on Long Island. The most prominent of these is the Long Island Greenbelt Trail Conference (23 Deer Path Road, Central Islip, NY 17222; 360–0753). The group's volunteer initiative has resulted in the opening of two major cross-island trails, the Long Island Greenbelt Trail, from Heckscher Park to Sunken Meadow Park, and the Nassau Suffolk Greenbelt Trail, from Massapequa to Cold Spring Harbor. Both follow preserves, parks, parkways, and other rights-of-way from shore to shore, mostly through woods and meadows and away from the obvious presence of suburbia. The Conference also has trail maps and guides and offers a regular program of guided hikes.

Farther east, in Suffolk, the nearly complete Pine Barrens Trail, which opens up major stretches through the unspoiled pine barrens areas both west and east of Riverhead, is being developed by the conference in conjunction with local authorities. On the south fork, two groups—the Southampton Trails Preservation Society (537–0660), and the East Hampton Trails Preservation Society (324–1127)—are busy laying out and linking trails to make many of the woods and preserves out there more accessible.

A hoped-for culmination of these efforts will be the Paumanok Path, a 100-mile hiking route envisioned to extend from Rocky Point on Long Island Sound, to Montauk Point. It is based in the west on the Pine Barrens Trail and on both new and existing trails east of the Shinnecock Canal. Since the Paumanok is an all-volunteer effort and the builders are faced with relatively few public lands along the route in the east, it may be some time before all the sections are linked together. In the meantime, consult with the agencies involved for current status.

It's worth noting that the East Hampton T.P.S. has an ambitious plan to complete their 40 odd miles of the Path by Oct. 1998. Considering their busy and diverse program of walks we think they may very well do it, thus giving Long Islanders more walking choices in this less spoiled part of the island.

The message we wish to make clear is that these blazed, linear trail systems are as much for our readers' benefit as they are for through-hikers. They exist so that we may all gain comfortable access to more nice places to walk.

While speaking of the pine barrens, it is appropriate to mention a recent development that may have a significant impact on their future. After years of arguing and litigation over the opposing views of developers, who desired little or no additional controls over land development there, and conservationists, who want little or no development at all in the 100,000-acre pine barrens area, an agreement was finally reached in June 1995 that seems workable and generally acceptable. As a result a 52,500-acre core area has become a forest preserve like the Catskills and Adirondacks, where development is essentially prohibited, while the peripheral lands will be open to controlled development. The basic environmental goals of preventing further loss of the once extensive pine-oak forest, of habitats for endangered plants and animals, and of watershed areas crucial for recharging our underground aquifers have been achieved. How this grand plan will work out in the face of future litigation remains to be seen, but it is clear that for our walking audience it augurs good things to come.

R.L.W.

Introduction

Walking is a pastime that can be carried out almost anywhere in city or country. Such a broad view of it, however, guarantees only to exercise your muscles. A nature walk, on the other hand, implies to us an event where exercise is secondary and the true goal is to relax and enjoy seeing and exploring new surroundings, to see more of the nonurban world and its flora and fauna. That's what we are hoping to bring you even on this busy island so close to New York City. We find that there are still many places where nature has held her own and, when man has cooperated, has prospered. We've walked here for years and recommend it.

If you are also interested in bird watching you may know that Long Island is one of the best places on the East Coast for that activity, principally for migratory birds. It is strategically located on a major flyway, and it has a wide variety of habitats that appeal to diverse species. A number of the walks in this book are associated with particular types of birds, and there are comments on those pairings. Although there are wide seasonal variations in the visiting populations, the best time for seeing them is in the Spring. That's when the birds are in their best plumage for breeding, and foliage has not yet reached full summer density.

Walking on Long Island deserves a few explanatory words, since it may be different from what you expect. It takes you into bracing air, clears your mind, and sharpens your senses. It's refreshing. You don't have to scramble up many hillsides or explore dangerous terrain. There is little need for blazes, and the only equipment needed is comfortable clothing and reasonably stout shoes. Of course, the birder mustn't fail to bring her binoculars nor the photographer his camera for there are abundant opportunities to use that kind of equipment.

Most of these places described in the pages that follow are best explored by two or three people, not groups. Also, it is usually the cars that are a problem ("where can we park legally?"). As a result many towns and villages, and the counties, have taken steps to limit access (parking) to the most popular recreation areas to local residents. This applies most strongly to the beaches and, to a lesser degree, parks. These restrictions, however, are enforced only from May to October (at most), when a permit to park is often required. At other times of the year access is open, and local inquiry will tell you when and where you can park. So be attentive, quiet, and courteous—and don't litter. You'll be welcome almost everywhere.

If these admonitions seem gratuitous—and indeed they might, with all the messages we receive today about litter and pollution—you will understand our deep concern as you take a closer look at our world. For as you move about on foot, you'll be constantly aware of both the fragility and the brave tenacity of nature. And because of the enjoyment you'll get from it, you'll want to admonish others to take care, too.

When you organize your walks, recognize that you may sometimes need to alter your plans because a particular area has become inaccessible or off-limits due to storm damage. This is most likely to apply to walks on or near the beaches, but occasionally woodland trails get blocked, too. Fortunately there are many alternative walks to be found almost everywhere on the island.

A word about hazards, none of which are too threatening, but still must be treated with caution. Equally annoying, and found in the same brushy areas, are thorny briers and poison ivy. Tough outer garments and through washing of exposed skin with soap and water are the best defense here.

A different situation arises with deer ticks. These tiny, pinhead-sized devils have become common in fields and woodland areas. Just brushing against vegetation allows the tick to join your walk and start moving along clothing to find a warm, soft patch of skin where it can burrow.

Not all of these ticks are infected with Lyme disease, as you can be bitten several times without having a problem. However, an untreated bite may have serious medical consequences if ignored. So, wear a hat, a light-colored, long-sleeved shirt, long pants, and long socks. Stretch the tops of the socks over the trouser legs to keep the ticks out, and use insect repellent.

This book is intended to give you seasonal walking choices. Perhaps in the height of summer you'll want to seek out the wooded, cooler places and walk the beaches when the swimmers have gone home. The towns also will be more appealing when the summer crowds have thinned.

But the fact is, taking a walk is almost always a good thing to do. If it's drizzling and overcast, it's a good day to walk; if it's cold or windy—or cold *and* windy—it's a good day to walk. Just dress appropriately. As Henry David Thoreau wrote, "When we walk, we naturally go to the fields and woods: what would become of us, if we walked only in a garden or a mall?"

The Atlantic Beaches

Long Island's best-known seashore is essentially a continuous, straight, 130-mile-long barrier beach of fine sand brought down over millennia as outwash from the two glacial moraines, Harbor Hill and Ronkonkoma, that form the forked backbone of the island. The beach sports some famous sections (Coney Island, Jones Beach, Fire Island, Montauk), some densely populated areas, and some miles of true seashore wilderness, but the beach is mostly distinguished by the different features along it, some man-made, some natural.

The ten sections we've chosen to highlight draw their character more from the people who use them in summer and from the nature of the communities behind the beach than from any physical differences. Every yard of the beach is the same, every yard is different; all of it is worth visiting, exploring, and remembering in all seasons of the year. Remember especially to visit in spring and fall when the bird migrations peak.

This brings up a necessary discussion about parking at the beaches. There are very few where parking is free year-round. State and county beaches usually have a charge for everyone from Memorial Day to Labor Day, with no restrictions the rest of the year. On the other hand, town and village beaches will usually have designated parking areas with signs saying PARKING BY PERMIT ONLY. These permits are normally available only to local residents, free or for a nominal charge. Nonresidents may be able to purchase one for a stiffer price.

The good news is that these permit restrictions are usually enforced only in the summer (perhaps May though October or June to September), so check locally for the exact dates. Out of season, anyone is welcome to use the beaches. You will also see, however, that most beach approach roads are liberally marked with NO PARKING signs. These are enforced all year, so be sure you end up in a "permit" lot. We have tried to identify them on the maps with the symbol Ⓟ.

Beach walks are rather hard to calibrate in terms of time and effort, though we have listed mileages in many cases. Hard sand exposed by the tide makes for fairly easy walking; soft sand above the tide line or on a sand road behind the beach can be very tiring. Since all these beach walks call for you to retrace your steps to get back to the car, it may be best to time your walks so you can use the hard sand both ways.

One other caution is in order. Remember that the dunes in back of the beach are the only barrier that prevents the ocean from washing over the top in a storm and destroying whatever is behind it. This has happened countless times in the past, and so all along the coast people are asked to keep off the dunes, except at formal crossings. This prevents harm to the beach grass that helps hold the dunes in place against erosion.

We've described these beach walks in order from west to east, like all the other parts of this book, simply to be orderly; enjoy them in any sequence!

Robert Moses State Park

Fire Island stretches 32 miles from Democrat Point on the west to Moriches Inlet on the east. This barrier island features one of the world's great beaches and has, besides seventeen small summer communities, one state park (Robert Moses), one county park (Smith Point), and a number of areas that form the bulk of the Fire Island National Seashore. U.S. Park Service visitor centers at Sailors Haven, Watch Hill, and Smith Point provide good opportunities to learn more about this delightful area, and the main office in Patchogue is the place to turn for information (289–4810).

Robert Moses State Park is the westernmost 875 acres of Fire Island and is reachable by car on either the Meadowbrook or Wantagh Parkways, across causeway and bridge that take you over Great South Bay and Fire Island Inlet to several parking fields accommodating more than 5,000 cars. It is parkway all 49 miles from New York City; the park is open sunrise to sunset.

Since this broad, flat beach is walkable any time of year, you will never be alone hiking. It is something of an adventure, because its ready accessibility draws a wide assortment of people attracted here by the sea, the sand, and the spaciousness of its open sky. But it is refreshing. Breathing air tempered by the sea, observing others reveling in the out-of-doors, and watching sandpipers scurry to the surf's edge then wheel away into the air

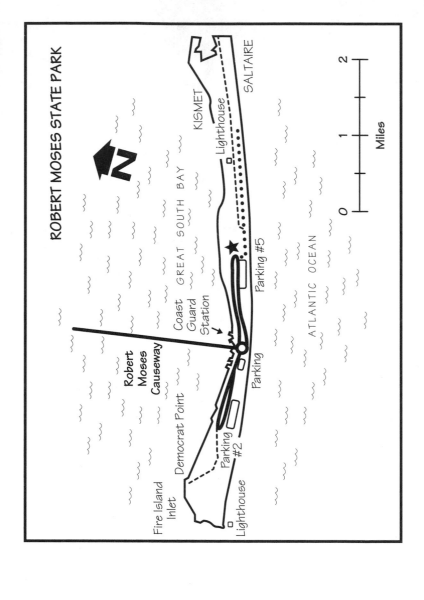

ROBERT MOSES STATE PARK

N

Fire Island
Inlet

Robert
Moses
Causeway

Democrat Point

Lighthouse

Parking
#2

GREAT SOUTH BAY

Coast
Guard
Station

Parking

Parking #5

KISMET

Lighthouse

SALTAIRE

ATLANTIC OCEAN

0   1   2

Miles

as you approach, will make time pass more quickly than you'd imagine. So look at your watch as you leave the parking area. There is uninterrupted beach ahead for more miles than you can walk today.

From the easternmost large parking lot (labeled field 5) the distances are:

East to the lighthouse 1.4 miles
East to Kismet (first Fire Island community) 2.1 miles
East to the Sunken Forest 6.7 miles
West to Democrat Point at Fire Island Inlet 3.4 miles

The beach, known for many years as Great South Beach, is indeed great, one of the finest beaches in the world. As you visit at different seasons, you will see that it changes size and shape, is cut away in winter, flattens out in summer. Erosion brings change, as does the longshore transport of sand by currents. The lighthouse, which was built in 1856, replaced the first one built at the western tip of the island in 1825, but the inlet is now 5 miles west of the light. The Corps of Engineers keeps dredging out the ship channel that separates it from the next island to the west, so Fire Island no longer actively grows westward.

For a short walk head out eastward. We clock ourselves, going for about an hour, then turn around and come back, and advise you to do the same. You will probably get to the light-house or a bit beyond.

If you do walk to the lighthouse, you will find a small museum (nominal fee) and can take a guided tour of the structure (by reservation—661–4876).

In September and October you are also likely to witness migrating hawks seeking food to power the next leg of their shoreline migration south. Local birders will be there, too, identifying and counting the travelers, and doing their observing mostly in the stretch between paved road and the lighthouse.

Perhaps it is best, if you seek solitude, to walk here after a storm or during the rain, when most people will not venture out.

But people flock together, and groups thin out as you go eastward.

There are refreshment stands, picnic shelters, and a bathhouse open in season. The park is open all year and has a $5.00 parking fee in the summer, and a $4.00 weekend fee in off season. Questions? Call 669-0449.

Sailors Haven
and Sunken Forest

The waves of the great Atlantic Ocean, set in motion 600 or more miles offshore by the wind, head westward unimpeded, slide up over the continental shelf, and, with almost hourly changes of mood, strike the Long Island South Shore beaches with pulsations of fascinating and hypnotic qualities. Their visual aspects change, too, so frequently in fact that there is never a dull day at the beach. There is never the threat of oppressive crowds. It is glorious. There is a fascination that nothing can quite describe, drawing you back again and again, refreshing you—and quietly luring you into spending an hour or a day longer than you had in mind.

We have come in the early spring, starting off in weather so thick we could not see Fire Island from the Sayville side, to have the sun later break through to show off the carpet of beach heather climbing these dunes, golden in bloom.

As the barrier beach built up, collecting more and more sand, the wind piled it up and formed these dunes. While some are only 4 or 5 feet high, many, as these here, reach a height of 35 or 40 feet.

Behind the dunes, between Cherry Grove and Point O' Woods, is a sanctuary well worth a visit that affords a pleasant walk. The Sunken Forest comprises almost forty acres of land. It is a short walk, close to Sailors Haven ferry dock. As you cross

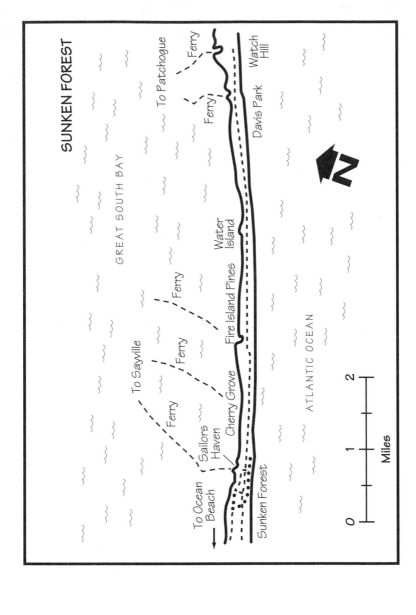

SUNKEN FOREST

GREAT SOUTH BAY

To Patchogue

Ferry

Ferry

To Sayville

Ferry

Ferry

Ferry

To Ocean
Beach

Sailors
Haven

Cherry Grove

Fire Island Pines

Water
Island

Davis Park

Watch
Hill

Sunken Forest

ATLANTIC OCEAN

N

Miles

0   1   2

to the south and climb the ramps protecting the dunes, you rise 35 feet above sea level and look across the top of the dunes to the Great South Bay beyond.

The dense vegetation between you and the bay is the top of the forest. Now rare, although there have been many similar forests in New Jersey as well as Cape Cod, the Sunken Forest of Fire Island has fortunately been preserved, and we are able to see here many trees that are estimated to be at least a hundred years old. The principal trees are American holly, shadblow, and sassafras, grown to a height of 35 to 40 feet. Normally these species do not reach this size because they are crowded out by stronger, taller-growing trees. Here, however, the red maple, red cedar, black and post oak, and pitch pine are themselves sheared off by the salty winds from the ocean and thus all are stunted to the protecting screen height of the dunes. The understory here was at one time a dense thicket of catbrier, Virginia creeper, and poison ivy that was alive with birds and small animals. However, the uncontrolled deer population has devastated the area by browsing on anything green, leaving only tree trunks and bare earth. As a result, almost all other animals, birds, and plants have vanished, and normal succession of trees seems very unlikely.

The boardwalk comes out on the bay side into almost blinding light if it is a bright day, through thickets of phragmites reeds, hugs the sandy shore, and reenters the forest to the west, twining back through the area. On a hot summer day it's pleasantly cool.

To reach Sailors Haven, take the ferry (passengers only—no cars) from River Road, Sayville. From May to November it usually operates on a regular schedule. After the summer season, service ends to Sailors Haven but continues all winter, on a limited basis, from Sayville to Cherry Grove and Fire Island Pines, which are 1 or 2 miles away on foot. Another option is to take the Ocean Beach ferry from Bay Shore—with a 3-mile walk. Call the ferries for schedules: 589–8980 in Sayville, 665–3600 in Bay Shore; or try the Sailors Haven ranger station at 597–6210 for more information.

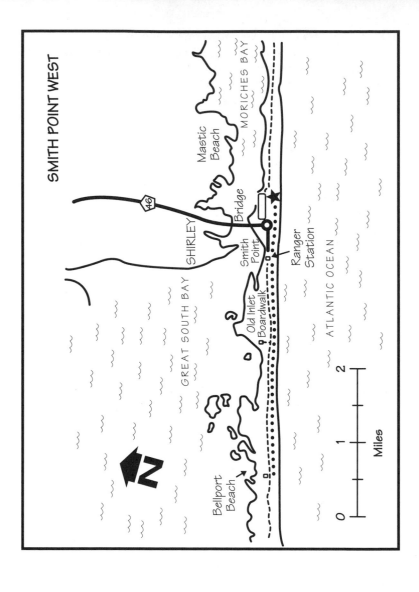

3

Smith Point

The beach accessible at Smith Point is one of our favorite places to walk, and the 7-mile stretch westward to Watch Hill is presently the only federal wilderness area in New York State and consequently is not open to vehicles (although specially permitted four-wheel-drive vehicles may drive on the ocean beach only). A causeway and bridge lead to the eastern end of the island, where there's ample parking. (The summer parking fee is $8.00 for non-Suffolk County residents and less for those who live in the county.) This is at the south end of the William Floyd Parkway. Train service on the Montauk line goes to Shirley Station, 2.5 miles from the bridge.

A two-story, octagonal visitor center on the dunes houses the National Seashore ranger's office (281–3010), which is open year-round and contains an informative display on beach life.

The beach westward offers a walk stretchable as far as you'll be able to go. We usually head for the Old Inlet, which is about a 2-mile round trip. The National Seashore maintains a shower–rest room building there during the summer and an ocean-to-bay boardwalk as well as a small dock with a buoy-marked channel leading to it. In moderate or cold weather it's nice to come back on the sand trail (formerly used as a road) that runs inland parallel to the ocean.

At low tide a colorful array of pebbles is exposed that may get you started on a pebble collection! White, black, red, brown, lavender, and those with subtle variations are available in a seemingly limitless supply. In fact, that's where all the sand comes from—the rocks and stones beat against each other, reducing themselves into smaller and smaller pieces. Scoop up these dry sands and, as they run through your fingers, investigate them carefully. At least half the sand is quartz, but there is hornblende, rutile, feldspar, augite, magnetite, ilmenite—a variety of names to confound you or just possibly to start you exploring a whole new world of minerals and rocks. Below Hatteras, down into the beaches of the south, much of the sand is made up of tiny shell fragments, but not here on Long Island. Shells are relatively scarce. The rocks that make up these beaches were brought by the mighty glaciers of the Ice Age all the way from Canada. So as you inspect the debris of the sand, you might find anything. They tell us specks of ruby and emerald exist here—but rarely! However, if you search, you'll certainly find garnet. And the black patches contain magnetite, an important iron ore that sometimes becomes magnetized; when it does, it's called lodestone. If you run a magnet through this, you'll find particles will cling.

With no people living on this thin stretch of the barrier beach, a walk here exposes some of the fragile links in the chain of life. For among the variety of life zones—the tidal edge of the sea, the beach itself, behind the sandy swales of the dunes, and in the wetlands along the Great South Bay—is a busy world to capture your interest and excite your imagination. We see hoofprints of deer here often, but deer are remarkable in becoming invisible. Only once or twice have we actually seen them here.

4

Quogue and Tiana Beaches

Cross the bridge at Quogue or Hampton Bays onto Dune Road. About midway between the two is Tiana Beach, where there's parking and easy access across the dunes.

Wide and open, the beach here is strung out with cottages just behind the dunes, but they don't dominate the landscape. We generally walk a mile west, by the round apartment complex and several summer places to the Quogue Public Beach, and return. Then we walk another mile east to total an hour and a half or two hours of elapsed time. It is never too crowded.

Low tide is the best time to walk on the beach because the wet sand is compact and settled by the waves. So all along the water's edge the firm walkway is hard enough not to hold you back in your own footsteps. Actually, water still remains between the individual grains of sand, and even on the hottest days the sun only dries the surface. There's a microscopic world of channels and ponds teeming with almost invisible life. Just watch the tiny sandpipers scurrying up to the water's edge, pecking away at the oozing sand. That's what they're after.

Quite apart from our walks, however, another reason compels us to come back here. That is Dune Road. The variety of shorebirds using the wetlands along the north of the road is almost endless. Almost all these creatures that nest or visit Long Island can be seen at some spot along here, wading in the shal-

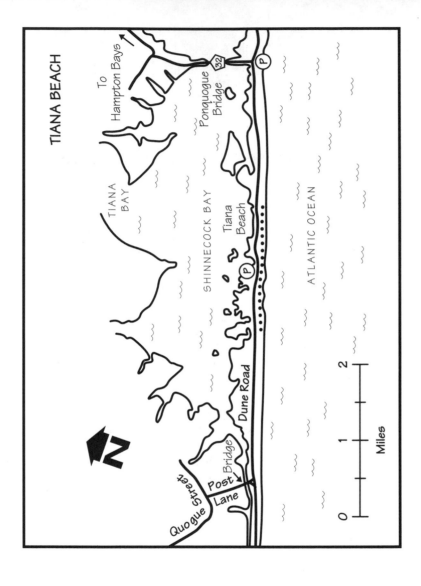

TIANA BEACH

To Hampton Bays

Ponquogue Bridge

32

TIANA BAY

SHINNECOCK BAY

Tiana Beach

ATLANTIC OCEAN

Dune Road

Post Bridge

Quogue Street

Lane

N

0   1   2

Miles

lows, standing in the grass, or winging low over the water. During the migratory season you will see one or two dunlin, black-bellied plover, ruddy turnstone, and then another and another, until you realize that the grass or shoreline is alive with them.

Come equipped with glasses and your bird guide. You'll find your car a perfect blind from which to observe. Drive along slowly. We've seen and heard the clapper rail, with his raucous call, and watched the bittern slowly swaying as he holds his bill in the air pretending to be a reed, trying to elude us. And we have watched black skimmer after black skimmer feeding, with their precision glide along the water. You'll see it all on Dune Road.

The slimy wetlands swarm with insects, and the water is unfit to drink. But acre for acre, the salt marsh will produce more plants than any farm, fertilizing itself, needing no help from man in planting or harvesting. Not only is it the feeding ground for the migrating birds you see along Dune Road, but it provides shelter and food for small mammals as well. We've watched the muskrat swimming here and working in the shallows, for example. And the tiny fish that swim and breed here are carried out on tides to feed still larger fish miles from shore. When you see the fill on some of this wetland, you realize that environmentalists do not always win the continuing battle with developers.

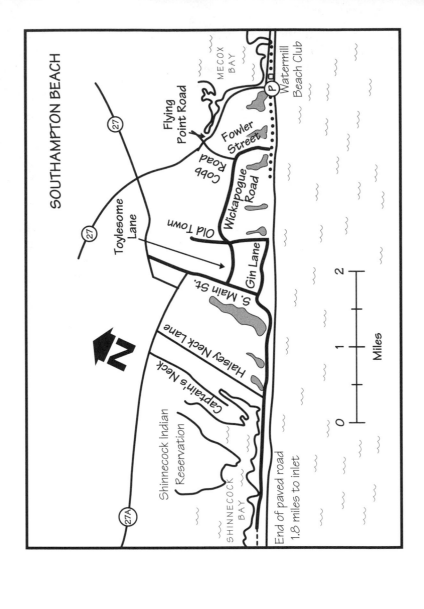

SOUTHAMPTON BEACH

MECOX BAY

Watermill Beach Club

Flying Point Road

Fowler Street

Cobb Road

Wickapogue Road

Toylesome Lane

Old Town

Gin Lane

S. Main St.

Halsey Neck Lane

Captain's Neck

Shinnecock Indian Reservation

SHINNECOCK BAY

End of paved road 1.8 miles to inlet

Miles

0   1   2

5

Southampton Beach

From the Shinnecock Inlet in Southampton eastward, the beach stretches in a broad unbroken swath for 11 miles to Sagaponack Pond. In summer this area attracts, for the most part, those who are content to lie out in the sun, dip in the magnificent surf— sometimes it's too magnificent and must be respected—and picnic or fling the Frisbee. Off-season it is almost completely uninhabited except for the occasional dog walker, surf fisherman, or bird watcher.

There are many public access areas where you may park. Sometimes there is a fee, or a parking permit is required (obtained at the Southampton Village or one of the town halls or at the beach). Out of season, however, there should be no problem.

This stretch is characterized by high dunes; rather large summer houses, usually set well behind the dunes for protection; a number of guarded beaches for swimming; good walking at low tide; and many ponds just behind the dunes where there is always more to see than a bird. At the east end of Shinnecock Bay, the beach ceases to be a barrier island (or here a peninsula) and all the rest of the way to Montauk becomes part of the mainland. These are classic beaches, the kind you see in marvelous color prints—the dunes covered with pale chartreuse grasses, the sun catching the movement of the waves, and a mist of salt spray hanging over the broad stretches of white sand.

At the Shinnecock or western end of this stretch there are no buildings at all, and the dunes are unusually high. Terns must nest here, for once in the spring they literally dive-bombed us. Parking out here is informal. The road peters out, so be careful unless you have a four-wheel-drive vehicle. The walk to the jetty is about 2 miles.

There are three or four other accesses to the beach. Our favorite section to walk is the one locally known as Fowlers. The approach to the high dunes is past a couple of ponds through broad potato fields, some seasons planted in wheat for rotation. Parking is in a lot off the road just before the dunes, so your walk is first to get to the beach. There are usually interesting birds on both sides of the ponds, and in August they are surrounded by huge pink or rose flowers of the marsh mallow. We turn left as we come onto the beach, walk along the water to Mecox Bay and back, making a total distance of just over 3 miles.

Beach walks clear your mind of many things. Often personal problems are replaced by other thoughts worth consideration, like the fact that geologists say these beaches are a million years old!

For a change of scene while in Southampton, it might be interesting to visit the Dupont Nature Sanctuary, at the southeast end of Captains Neck Lane. It harbors a true salt-marsh ecosystem that forms a kind of natural barrier between ocean and land. It provides a resilient buffer against the forces of storm and tide, but most importantly, it represents the first link in the food chain. This is where organic matter decays to feed even larger organisms, from plankton to fish to people.

6

Wainscott Beach

Of the five unbroken stretches of beach along Long Island's south shore, Wainscott Beach, 3.6 miles from end to end, is the shortest. Many walkers have a compulsion to cover every mile of a stretch, just because it is there, and it's easy to understand the urge because it is satisfying to traverse any stretch. Still, on the broad, flat strands of the coastline here, there aren't any startling discoveries. One beach is very much like another. There are differences, of course, but these differences are subtle, sometimes more metaphysical than real. And since, from hour to hour, aspects of the beach walking experience change anyway, it can be misleading to describe any of Long Island's beaches in specific detail. Wainscott Beach is probably the most out-of-the-way. There are cottages all along, well back in grassy stretches, and the dunes are lower. For some reason driftwood does not accumulate here to the extent it does farther east. Freighters at sea seem farther out.

To reach Wainscott Beach, turn south from the Montauk Highway 1.3 miles east of Bridgehampton on Sagg Main Street to Sagaponack, and on to the end; or go to the end of Beach Lane in Wainscott.

It's a good idea to check the tide tables before you start off and try to do your principal walking during low tide, when the footing is more solid and the walking easier! Up on the higher

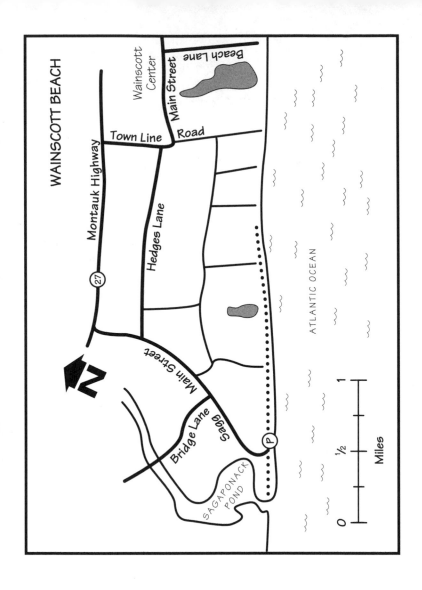

ground the surface sand does dry to a greater depth, and walking becomes more laborious.

When you stand on the beach facing the sea, you can notice from many little indicators that the water pulls to the west. For the longest time we simply couldn't understand this. We'd say that the Gulf Stream was out there moving eastward and northward along the coast, so how could the water here along shore move as it obviously does, in the opposite direction? Have you asked yourself this question? Have you seen how the sand moves west with the currents, how pieces of driftwood move back toward New York? In a word, the answer is friction. The Gulf Stream is a very large river, about 40 miles wide and 2,000 feet deep, with a volume of water a thousand times larger than our biggest river, and it moves about 5½ miles per hour in a northeasterly direction. As it moves, the water along the shore is set into counter-currents and eddies that flow for a time in the reverse direction because of the friction of the shore.

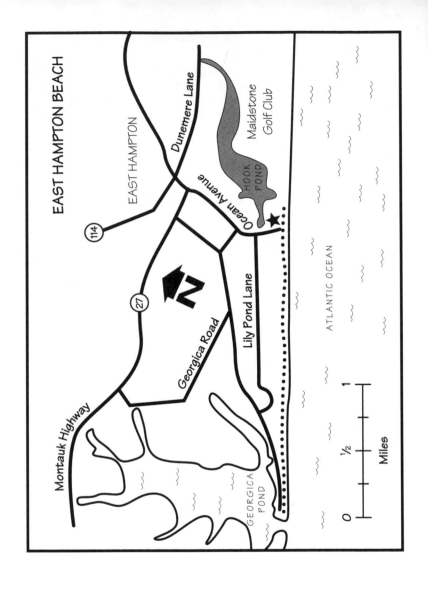

EAST HAMPTON BEACH

EAST HAMPTON

Dunemere Lane

114

Maidstone Golf Club

HOOK POND

Ocean Avenue

27

N

Montauk Highway

Georgica Road

Lily Pond Lane

GEORGICA POND

ATLANTIC OCEAN

0   ½   1
Miles

7

East Hampton Beach

From Georgica Pond the Long Island South Beach is uninterrupted for 22.2 miles to Montauk. Locally the stretch is referred to as East Hampton Beach, Amagansett Beach, Napeague Beach, or Montauk Beach, depending on its proximity to the adjoining community. The entire stretch is magnificent and eminently walkable.

Parking on East Hampton beaches is restricted to residents only during the season. The Town of East Hampton is chic, beautifully maintained, and handsome because of tree-shaded lanes and many attractive houses. It has a casual dignity and considerable local civic pride. We've driven along streets here early in the morning, before breakfast, on the way to the beach and seen golden pheasant, one after another, strutting across village greenswards. This pastoral, relaxed village atmosphere is the secret of East Hampton's jealously guarded charm, and a strong effort is being made to keep it this way.

A good walk on East Hampton Beach is from the village beach east of Hook Pond; walk westward to the Georgica Pond inlet and return. The total distance, round-trip, is 6.4 miles. On your right as you head out will be the Maidstone Golf Club and Hook Pond, which is a good birding area. Beyond Main Street Beach the dune area is fairly primitive, low and windswept. Off-season you can find a place to park.

The beach here is in striking contrast to, say, the beaches west of Jones Beach, where our urban sprawl has crowded out the dunes. The charm and attractiveness of Eastern Long Island is threatened by growth—the statistically predictable population explosion and overcrowding that seem inevitable. East Hampton is vigorously trying to preserve its heritage, limit its growth, and save its open land for living space. As you walk Long Island, you will appreciate its openness, see the need to save its wild areas, but feel the pressures crowding in to crush its rural character. You may feel yourself helpless as an individual in a crowded society and wonder what you can do to help in conserving this. The answer might be to become involved, to work with others, such as The Nature Conservancy, for a common end. The administration of our civic affairs apparently works under pressure of an aroused citizenry.

8

Amagansett Beach

An easy direct access to Amagansett Beach is to turn south off the Montauk Highway on Indian Wells Highway (2.5 miles east of East Hampton, but before you reach Amagansett). At its end is a bathhouse on the east side, and opposite this, Sheppard's Dunes, an eight-acre area acquired and protected by The Nature Conservancy to preserve its natural state. Parking during the season is reserved for residents. It's better to walk in late spring or early fall anyway.

The beach itself has character. Houses sit almost half a mile up from the beach on bluffs overlooking the sea, and the dunes are wild. So our suggestion is to walk to Maidstone Golf Club, which is 2.5 miles to the west on the wide beach, then return.

For anyone who has lived in inland wooded areas, the plants and ground cover of the seashore offer a fascinating world of discovery. When there's a break in the dunes, as there is here, you can be tempted to cross in order to examine interior plant life. But don't do it. You will crush the dune grasses, making the passage vulnerable to wind erosion. And just one such spot can actually weaken an entire dune. So be conservation minded and alert to damage to any plant life. You will be able to find a path allowing you to observe.

The beach grass, with its long, curving leaves, is the principal stabilizer for the dunes. It gets its nourishment from wind-blown

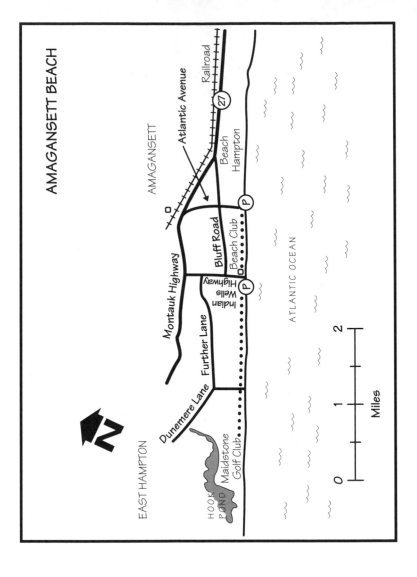

minerals, grows up, sends its roots deep, and follows the contours of the dunes. The false heather is another, with bright buttery yellow blossoms from May through July. It is a low, shrubby plant adapted to life on the shifting sands.

Just over the dunes, when there's soil enough, the beach pea will take hold, send its vinelike leaflets swarming, the ends with little tendrils like a pig's tail. You will want to examine the pea flowers, which are delicate in shades of violet and purple, blossoming throughout the summer. Inland, thickets of beach plum and bayberry take hold with beautiful fruit in the fall.

When the dunes are stabilized, the exuberance that nature displays is amazing. Above all, you should beware of poison ivy, rampant near the beach. You will find rugosa rose, seaside goldenrod, thistle, and blueberry. It is really quite startling to realize the wide variety of plant life near the beach.

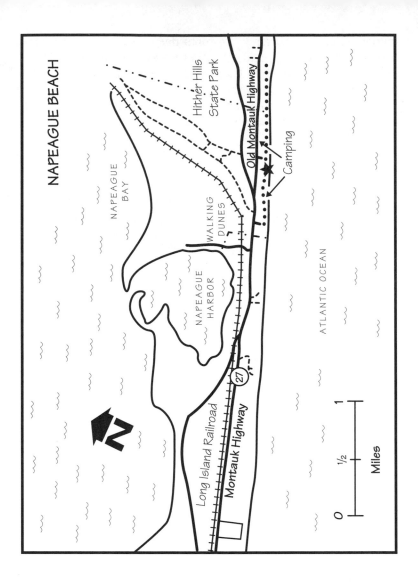

9

Napeague Beach

After you leave Amagansett, driving east, the ocean comes into view from the highway for the first time. The peninsula abruptly narrows; two bodies of water—Napeague Bay and Harbor—extend southward, making the land here less than a mile wide until you reach Hither Hills (about 6 miles). The road parallels the ocean about a half mile inland. The land is flat with low dunes and familiar seaside plants. Napeague Beach extends eastward from Amagansett. It's easiest to get onto the beach through the Hither Hills State Park.

This is a good place to get a feeling for the forces that shaped Long Island's topographical features. As you leave Amagansett you see the high dunes petering out; then at Hither Hills the land mass piles up again, now in contours and hills that are more than 150 feet above sea level. The land masses are the result of the moraine pushed here by the glaciers and modified ever since by the continuous action of wind and sea. Great rolling breakers have been moving in on the Long Island shoreline for a million years since the first glacier came down, and for more than 25,000 years since the last, scooping up rocks and sand, rubbing and grinding, and depositing the very fine particles that form the present continuous beach. And the wind has blown it around. What with storms and tides and longshore transit of sands by currents, there have been constant changes in elevations and shorelines. It is recorded that there were seven inlets east of Fire Island in 1743—but then Fire Island was 55 miles long. It was not until 1931 that big waves and high tides separated the dunes and broke through Fire Island at Moriches Inlet in a destructive storm. And it is inevitable that there will be further change.

As you walk the Napeague Beach, go east for a time and see the high bluffs where the Ronkonkoma Moraine comes right to the sea. Turn around and walk past the park to the low dunes. Along the way you will surely see a fisherman or two.

Offshore the bottom is even and shoals quite gradually, and you will generally see commercial and sport fishing boats trolling along here as the fishing is apt to be good. At least surfcasters have this attitude. During the summer there are schools of bluefish, sea bass, porgies, and flounder. Late in the autumn striped bass can be caught and, through the winter, cod.

10

Montauk Beach

There's a gap in the morainal hills that defines Montauk Beach—about a 3.5-mile stretch of broad sandy beach below the high dunes along the Old Montauk Highway. East of this you come to the 70-foot-high bluffs, a kind of land's end, halfway between New York City and the farthest reach of Cape Cod, which is Montauk Point. Kirk Park Beach, right in town, is a popular spot all year, since access is easy and the beach is nice and wide. There will be bathers and people lying in the sun if it's summer. And if you walk west toward the dunes, you should surely see surfers in wet suits, because the conditions are evidently good there.

For a less busy area with bluffs you can walk on; go about a mile east on Route 27 and turn down Ditch Plains Road to reach the town beach there. It's a fine, wide strand, too, but if you head west on footpaths just in back of the low bluff, you'll soon be high enough for dramatic views of the beach below, the higher bluffs east to Montauk Point, and, close at hand, a few of the long, overgrown "buildings" that were gun emplacements for coastal defense during World War II.

The best surfing waves are known as spilling breakers—those that, as they approach the beach, have a line of foam spilling down their front, always just about to break but holding off for quite a while. Since the more gradual the slope of the bottom, the longer the wave will hold off breaking, so it stands that

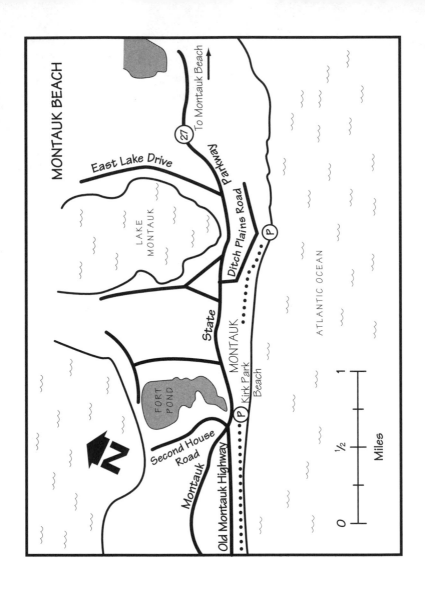

the best surfing is on the kind of beach that has a long stretch underwater with almost no slope at all.

There is never a day on these waters when there is no surf whatsoever, though it is possible for it to be too dull for those who make a sport of it. The whole science of waves is complex, but it is interesting to know that a wave will break when the ratio of the height of the wave to the depth of water is about three to four; that is to say that a 6-foot wave will break in about 8 feet of water.

The wave action is caused principally by the wind's force against the surface of the water. The water itself actually moves very little. You can see this when you watch a cork or piece of driftwood bobbing at sea; after the wave has passed, you see how little the cork has moved. When a wave passes through very shallow waters, it lifts and stirs up sand from the bottom, so the loose grains of sand settle in a different place than where they started. That's how waves change and shape the contours of beaches.

The changes in the beach would not, most likely, startle the Montauk Indians, whose name it bears. The Montauks, who were so naturally protected here from their mainland enemies, made quantities of wampum on these beaches from the shells of periwinkles and quahogs. No, these changes would not startle them half as much as the changes on land, where the indigenous hardwoods of New England—beech, oak, and maple—and the 140- or 150-foot tulip trees from which they fashioned their canoes have all been destroyed.

Towns to Explore on Foot

One of the joys of walking is to step out of the fetters of time, to while away and unwind at a leisurely pace and with a certain detachment. Keeping alert to the surroundings in this carefree state, you'll experience a feeling of satisfaction. Walking along the edge of the sea may give you a sense of leaping back in time, and walking along narrow streets of an old village may make you feel nostalgic, feeding your hankering for a simpler life.

Long Island was colonized by New Englanders, mostly from Connecticut, and English architectural influences are visible in a number of places, some dating as far back as the Old House in Cutchogue (1649). There are Dutch influences, too, which pushed eastward from New Amsterdam.

Rural village charms that still exist on Long Island are mainly left over from the nineteenth century. By then the settlements had established a character that has strong appeal to us today. There are other communities you might want to explore besides the six we describe here. They offer interesting architecture and still retain vestiges of rural village charms. We suggest you try to investigate *Amityville*, south of Farmingdale at the end of Broad Hollow Road and south of the Sunrise Highway; *Roslyn Park*, just south of North Hempstead Turnpike between Port Washington Boulevard and Glen Cove Road; and the hamlet of *Oyster Bay*, all in Nassau County. And in Suffolk County, visit *Cold Spring Harbor*, on North Hempstead Turnpike, 2 miles west of Huntington; and *Northport*, east of Huntington and Centerport, north of Route 25A. There's an old pre-Revolutionary church on Main Street at the Setauket Green in *Setauket*, west and north of Port Jefferson.

Riverhead is also a town worth visiting, but not for New England charm, which is largely absent. The real reason to visit is the small but excellent Suffolk County Historical Society Museum at 300 West Main Street. It houses a unique collection of artifacts reflecting more than three centuries of change. Household objects and furniture, Native American items, farm and maritime tools, and buggies and carts provide an honest glimpse of Long Island's history. It is worth noting that Riverhead is very convenient for accessing nearly half of the walks we have listed. The museum is open Tuesday, Wednesday, Thursday, and Saturday from 12:30 to 4:30 P.M., but phone before going to be sure it's open (727–2881). Admission is free, donations are welcome, and the gift shop has an unparalleled variety of books about Long Island.

Douglas Manor

Douglas Manor is a community of cozy-looking houses set on a peninsula that juts into Little Neck Bay at the eastern end of Queens County. It is that part of Douglaston that lies entirely north of the tracks of the Port Washington Branch of the Long Island Rail Road, and we think you would really enjoy the walk around the peninsula, along a sidewalk by the water's edge much of the way. If you come by train, get off at the Douglaston station. By car, leave Northern Boulevard on Douglaston Parkway and head north past the station area until you find a place to park. That may mean looking for several blocks, especially during the week, when commuters are here in numbers.

Start your walk on the west side by going down 36th Avenue to the shore road and then heading north along Little Neck Bay. In the summer this is a very popular place for shorebirds and modest sailboats. The waters are unusually clean, largely due to the total absence of commercial activities and marinas. Once you round the north point and head down Marinette Street and Douglas Road, you'll be on the edge of a small park and a large, marshy wildlife preserve that extends over to the far shore. To return to your starting point from the end of Douglas Road, just turn right on Hillside Avenue and continue over the hill to West Drive. The total walking distance, starting at the station, is about 2.5 mostly level miles.

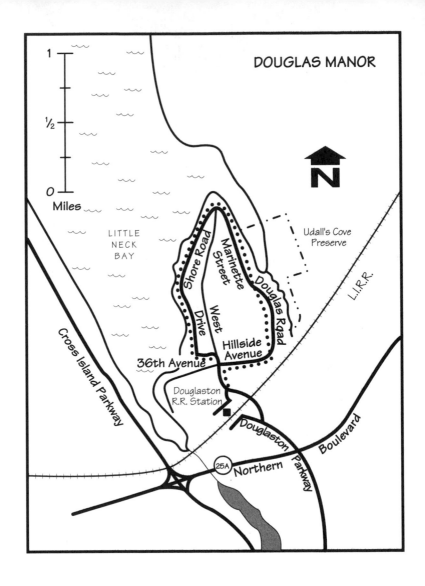

If you take the additional time to explore the streets of Douglas Manor, which we recommend, you will quickly sense that it is an unusual community. Although there are a few old houses, one dating to 1732, the town's history dates from around 1906, when the Douglas estate was developed into a railroad or "garden" suburb, and planned according to a radical notion at the time: cooperative ownership of the mile-long waterfront. The 590 houses represent every architectural style of the early twentieth century, including Queen Anne, Colonial, Tudor, and Mediterranean Revival, and range from virtual cottages to mansions. Many enjoy fine water views.

Recognition as a special place has also come through its designation by the city as one of New York's historic districts.

There has always been a strong bent here for community improvement, as evidenced by the fact that it has the largest community garden club in New York State. In another sense Douglas Manor is nearly an arboretum, because well over one hundred varieties of trees have been introduced over the years. The streets are graced by innumerable giants, topped by a 600-year-old white oak at 233 Arleigh Road. Many rare and exotic varieties are also to be found.

All in all there is much to catch your eye here—not only the water traffic one would expect on the sound and in the bay, but also the wildlife, which is abundant for so densely populated a county.

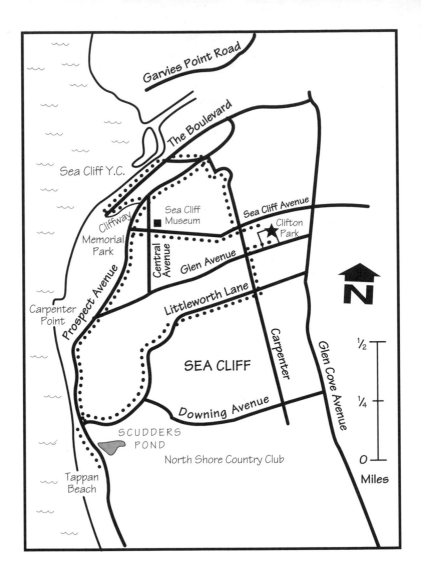

Sea Cliff

"The style of the houses in Sea Cliff," says one local resident with a measure of civic pride, "is what we call 'Carpenter Gothic.'" Perhaps this sets in your mind's eye a village that is a collection of highly individual gingerbread houses that have been lovingly attended to over the years. Actually there's an ample supply of larger, well-maintained Victorian ones as well, not to mention a real diversity in more modern varieties. You should enjoy a walk in Sea Cliff for surprises! It rolls comfortably over high bluffs overlooking Hempstead Harbor. Narrow streets running up and down steep slopes, some very small parcels of land, and loving care are the complementary parts that make up a whole picture of Sea Cliff that forms as you trudge around the town on foot.

Start off by parking near Clifton Park and walk westward along Sea Cliff Avenue. There are some big houses here, and you'll cross through the business district, perhaps quickly sensing that the principal industry these days is selling antiques. When you reach Central Avenue, detour briefly around to the north side of the Village Hall (former Methodist Church) to visit the Sea Cliff Museum. It is the community's response to the unique historical background of the town and has interesting artifacts and photographs from the past. An interesting booklet called *This is Sea Cliff* describes the background of the village, the many parks, and other points of interest. It costs $2.00, and it can also be bought in the Village Hall during normal business hours (671–0080). Hours for the museum are Saturday and Sunday from 2:00 to 5:00 P.M. (January and February from 2:00 to 4:00 P.M.), closed in the summer. For more information call 671–0090.

Return to Sea Cliff Avenue and continue on it. Shortly you will reach Memorial Park, site of an old inn, which was seized and demolished by the town for back taxes. The property is on the heights, and you will come upon a grand view of Long Island Sound.

Walk north on Prospect Avenue, left down Cliffway, and north again on The Boulevard. Two sets of steps will bring you back up to Prospect. A longer alternate walk is to go from Memorial Park south down Prospect Avenue to the shoreline and follow it as it curves along under the lovely old plane trees (sycamores) to Scudders Pond. Returning, you can explore the narrow streets along Sea Cliff's "Cliff Side" by following Littleworth Lane back up to Carpenter, thence along it to Glen Avenue and the park.

The first gathering of people here was really a Methodist summer camp meeting with tents, picnics, and summer smiles on faces of earnest city folk, singing hymns on the wooded hills above the water, away from the ruffians of the city. That was in 1865. Good steamboat service to New York City was available and convenient from the pier in the harbor. The church group later bought 240 acres from the Carpenter family, who owned the farmlands, and divided it. The atmosphere was so congenial that people eventually built little houses on their 40-by-60-foot lots to make the camp more permanent and lavished every spare dollar they could to make it attractive.

By 1895, however, word of its charms having spread, Sea Cliff had become a very popular summer resort, and many large Victorian houses had been built. There was a cable car up the cliff, and a boardwalk had been built along the shorefront. The Long Island Rail Road was running trains into the little gingerbread station on a regular schedule, spring, summer, and fall, and there were four boats daily between Sea Cliff and New York. Today it stands as one of the best-preserved little square miles around.

13

Old Bethpage Village Restoration

Unlike the other communities, Old Bethpage Village is a restoration, a composite made up of simple houses and shops with some architectural merit, regrouped here on a 200-acre site ample enough to provide a proper setting for the buildings and re-create the atmosphere of a mid-nineteenth-century village. And it is a pleasant surprise. We think it makes a delightful walk, a lovely switch in centuries.

You will find a parking lot and a reception center of contemporary design, as well as an adequate cafeteria, an excellent gift shop, and a small auditorium showing a film on the restoration. A $5.00 admission fee is charged, with reductions for senior citizens and children. Allow a couple of hours and spend another if you can make the time.

We walked into the days before the mechanization of the farm. This illusion is skillfully achieved. The dirt path we followed is bordered by a post-and-rail fence; the field through which it ambled lay fallow, but liberally sprinkled with Queen Anne's lace and butterflies. Birds chirped. There was the faint, not unpleasant, organic smell that emanates from a farmyard.

We were greeted at one of the houses by an eager youth who showed us through what had once been a bayman's dwelling.

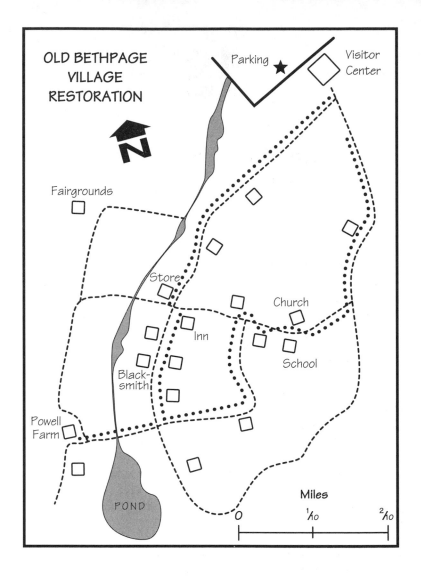

OLD BETHPAGE
VILLAGE
RESTORATION

N

Parking ★

Visitor
Center

Fairgrounds

Store

Church

Inn

School

Black-
smith

Powell
Farm

POND

Miles

0   1/10   2/10

Uncluttered, simply furnished, it set an informal, friendly air to our visit. Altogether forty-five buildings, all original structures, have been saved from destruction and moved here to form a charming nineteenth-century village.

At the crossroads is a general store, with the proprietor's living quarters under the same roof, an inn serving root beer in the Tap Room, and a blacksmith's forge. By this time we had noticed that all the guides were dressed in clothes of the period. It is not correct to say that they were wearing costumes—the garb is simple, functional, and doesn't at first catch your eye.

The Powell farm is functioning. There are pigs and cows, chickens and geese. The ladies were baking bread, and a pot of soup hung simmering from the crane over coals smoldering away in the fireplace. It was vegetable soup, and the gardens had provided all the ingredients. The flies buzzed, a Canada goose honked, and the old sow lay sprawled out in the mud.

It is an uncluttered, friendly, helpful little valley, and the attitudes of all the people working here make it so.

The walk around the loop is 1.5 miles. During the school year we were told there are daily groups—so our suggestion is to come, as we did, on a summer's day. Let the natural breezes provide the stream to float your daydreams on. Lengthen your stride, but slow down your pace, and reflect how downright simple the necessities of life can be. The 1.5-mile walk plus the other exploring footsteps will add up to enough on a hot afternoon.

Remember, though, that the village is open and alive all year (except in January and February), with daily hours from 10:00 A.M. to 5:00 P.M.; so it is possible to experience a variety of activities having to do with the passing of the seasons. For specific schedules and information, call 572–8400.

The entrance to the village is on the east side of Round Swamp Road, about 1 mile south of the Long Island Expressway (Route 495), exit 48.

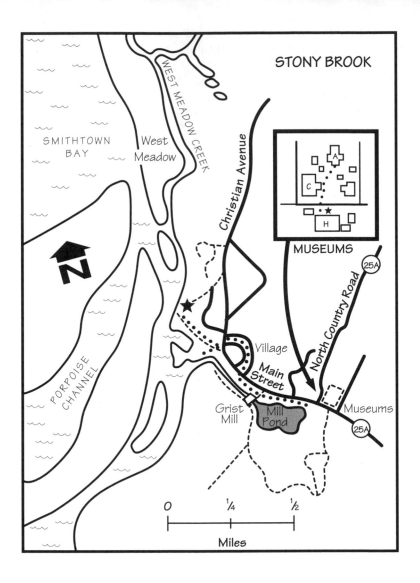

Stony Brook

Because Stony Brook village is old and handsome, we think you should see it for its unique charm and Long Island bayside country atmosphere.

Visitors will be interested in the complex of buildings now known as The Museums at Stony Brook. Founded in the 1930s, the museums comprise the largest privately supported museum group on Long Island. They include three major exhibition buildings and a number of eighteenth- and nineteenth-century historic structures. Their overall theme is the exhibition and interpretation of American art and history. Thus, in the Margaret Melville Blackwell History Museum (H) there are special exhibitions on historical themes, a gallery of period rooms (in miniature), and a superb collection of antique decoys. The Art Museum (A) also features changing shows, along with permanent displays of works by William Sidney Mount (1807–1868), the celebrated Long Island genre painter.

The original heart of the complex is now known as the Ward and Dorothy Melville Carriage House (C). It displays more than one hundred vehicles illustrating the history of horse-drawn transportation. The carts, cabs, coaches, broughams, phaetons, wagons, sleighs, and fire engines are all a delight to see. A "Pleasure Driving" section is but one of nine that help make this one of the finest such collections in the country.

When you visit Stony Brook (take Route 25A north from Smithtown), you can park either at the museums or on the waterfront. If you choose the former, go first to the History Museum (H) for admission tickets ($4.00 for adults). After seeing the three main buildings, you can also visit the blacksmith shop and schoolhouse. Be sure to leave enough time to walk north along Main Street about a half mile into the village, passing the Mill Pond with its resident families of waterfowl and water lilies, and stopping at the interesting old grist mill, which is in full operation. It is open from April through December; phone the Ward Melville Heritage Organization, formerly known as the Community Fund, which owns it, at 751–2244 for exact days and hours.

As you come to the village green, you'll find a variety of interesting shops up on the right, and the waterfront ahead on the left. The bay and salt meadows here supply as New England a scene as you might imagine. It is not difficult to see how the English settlers who came here from Suffolk chose these shores or why it reminded them of their native country. It's also easy to understand the overwhelmingly important part played by the sea, bays, and water routes in the first 200 years of Long Island's development.

If you can, take time to enjoy a trip around the harbor and wetlands for a seaman's view from the *Discovery.* Its schedule depends on the tides, so it is constantly changing. For reservations call 751–2244.

Stony Brook village is clean and tidy and has an air of nostalgia. You can walk along, window-shopping and dating old houses as you head to your starting point, but surely you will have lost track of time on the way.

Although the museums are open all year, both hours and admission fees are subject to change. We suggest that you telephone in advance (751–0066) to get current information on hours and special exhibitions.

Sag Harbor

Sag Harbor, a National Historic District, is certainly one of the best-preserved old villages on Long Island, with hedges and picket fences and curving, crooked, and shaded streets that are lined with charming houses.

Starting at the Chamber of Commerce windmill on the waterfront, walk along Bay Street and on to the Long Wharf, observe the coastal activity, inspect the windmill on Main Street at the waterfront, shop at any one of the numerous little stores and markets in the area, or stroll in the Marine Park or yacht club area. If you wish, look across the harbor from the North Haven Bridge to Shelter Island in the north. Then walk up Main Street as far as you like. The finest example of Greek Revival architecture in New York State, built in 1845, now houses the revitalized Whaling and Historical Museum (725–0770), which attracts more than 35,000 people seasonally. (It is open daily from May 15 through the end of September.) Across Garden Street is the Hannibal French House, a large Victorian mansion, now painted a pleasant, dark ivory color, and the old Custom House, which is a National Landmark and the home and office of the first customs collector of New York State. Sag Harbor was named an official Port of Entry in 1789 by President George Washington, and a U.S. Post Office was initiated by Postmaster General Benjamin Franklin.

On side streets—wander off on any of them—you'll see many

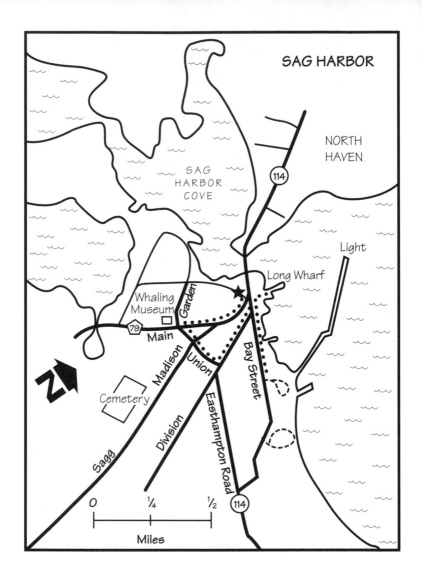

fine little houses built during prosperous days, late-eighteenth to mid-nineteenth century. They have simple lines in the style of that era. These residential streets have been restored with care, painted, and nicely planted by their present owners, giving you an indication of the prosperity of the past.

You should turn left at the museum and go along Union Street past Madison to see the First Presbyterian Church of Sag Harbor—locally known as the Whalers Church—based on Egyptian style and something of a curiosity. The spyglass-shaped steeple that once dominated the town was blown down in the hurricane of 1938 and never replaced. All the architectural trim is said to be hand-carved by whalers from the village. And nearby, the old graveyard is interesting. A lovelier-looking church is Christ Episcopal farther down Madison.

First there was a little fishing village started here in 1665 by a small band of Narragansetts, traditional rivals of the Montauks and Shinnecocks. Then the white settlers moved in around 1707. Although known for a time as Sterling Bay (after the English Lord Sterling), it eventually took the name Sag Harbor, being the harbor of Sagg, a little settlement near what is now Bridgehampton, a corruption of the native name Saggabonac: "Where the Ground Nuts (Potatoes) Grow!"

At the end of the eighteenth century, Sag Harbor cleared a greater tonnage of goods than New York Harbor, and it was to become one of the principal whaling ports on the Atlantic seacoast, second only to New Bedford. Between 1790 and 1870 more than 500 voyages were made from here, and the whale oil brought back to light the cities and houses of New England was valued at $25 million. There were once sixty-three vessels registered here. The population reached 3,500 by 1843. Rough seamen walked these very streets you roam today—Montauk and Shinnecock Indians, but also Fijians, Hawaiians, Malays, Ethiopians, and Portuguese.

After the Civil War the whaling industry had a rapid decline, and Sag Harbor's fortunes dwindled. Today, tourism and light manufacturing are a boon.

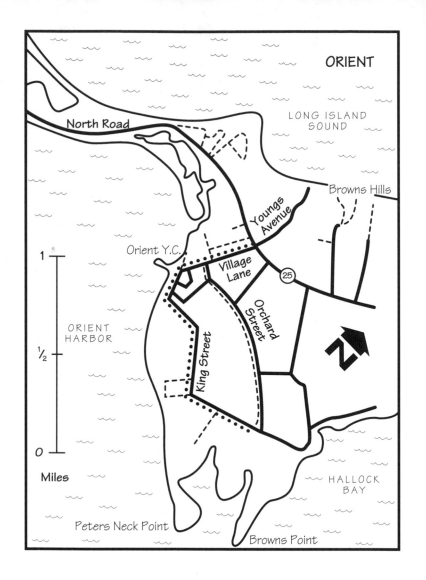

16

Orient

Places on earth, like people, seem to develop under current conditions along conforming lines. One airport looks pretty much like any other, anywhere in our world, and cities and houses fall into similar categories. Those places that guard their character from external forces and preserve their antiquities, develop an aura that is often admirable. Little villages lying somewhere along headwaters tend to preserve this aura, and the hamlet of Orient, lying the farthest east of any of the settlements on the northern fork, quite off the beaten track, has perhaps the greatest individuality of any place on Long Island.

We hope, in saying this, that anyone will cautiously consider the trust we place in he who reads this. Don't rush right out to look. A swarm of people would be out of place in Orient. It also is a simple place; you won't be overwhelmed! The houses aren't as grand as those in Southampton or East Hampton. Property plots are rather small, and the antiques are not on a scale that would attract Sotheby's. It is not quaint, and there are no shops of any kind, other than a small general store and post office, closed Sundays. So you might be disappointed. But for us, Orient has a special character all its own.

If you go, you will leave Greenport on Route 25. The town of East Marion is 2 or 3 miles, and 3 miles beyond that, just after you cross the narrow causeway with Long Island Sound on your left and Orient Harbor on your right, is the road (Village Lane) that leads down into the village. As you come to this causeway, you should stop at the parking place along the harbor, get out, and look. The map lays out well before you here. The village, from the distance, seems like one you'd see in Vermont. There are snowy white egrets that nest in the salt meadows and a peacefulness laid down on all the scene. We have read that Orient until after World War I was a favorite spot for honeymooners. Today it is primarily a quiet resort town.

Don't try to drive into town. Park off the road near the war memorial obelisk and the white church with the graceful steeple, at the head of the lane. If you do drive through, note the NO PARKING signs that alternate from one side to the other. Then walk along the Village Lane sidewalk. Houses, gardens, trees, and reflections will catch your eye. Orient has more than one hundred buildings built more than a century ago. Down the quiet, narrow, meandering Village Lane are the Oyster Ponds Museums, a six-building museum complex that is run by the Oyster Ponds Historical Society (323–2480). The first building is the Village House Museum, a simple clapboard structure with a long widow's walk. It has Early American furnishings and local collections and is clearly worth a visit. Behind it is the Hallock House with marine art, artifacts, and tools. Next door is the Old Schoolhouse; across the street, the Webb House. Then there is the Red Barn, and so on.

The museum buildings are open on Saturday and Sunday from 2:00 to 5:00 P.M. from the end of June through September, and also on Wednesday and Thursday in July and August. Admission is $3.00.

After visiting the museum group, continue down the lane by the yacht club, and you can lengthen the walk as we do by continuing on out into the country fields and swinging back by a loop into the village.

Woodlands, Parks, and Preserves

The idea of finding a pleasant trail winding through quiet woods or open fields may seem hard to accept on this island of 2.6 million people in Nassau and Suffolk counties, yet the reality is that there are miles and miles of such walks to be enjoyed. Only a few are listed in this section, forming a starting point for further exploration. They are mostly in fairly large areas that have been saved from being paved with roads and houses by state or county acquisition and/or by The Nature Conservancy. The woods, roads, and trails are used by walkers, horseback riders, cyclists, birders, and joggers as an escape from urban pressures, and they serve this purpose well. Other sections in this volume list similar walks; the ones here are primarily those where water is not a prominent part of the scene.

Many of these areas have extensive trail networks that offer a great deal of variety in the details you can observe as well as in the flora and fauna. Others have nature trails, usually self-guiding, that can provide more points of interest in a short distance than would be expected from simply wandering down an old road through a scrub oak woodland. In still others you'll find a long-distance trail passing through that, while interesting, doesn't lend itself to a loop walk to take you back to your starting point over new terrain. As a consequence, while we've highlighted the walks that seem best for first acquaintance, do try others that show on our maps or on the maps that are often available at the park or preserve. We think you'll enjoy the variety, especially if you visit during different seasons of the year.

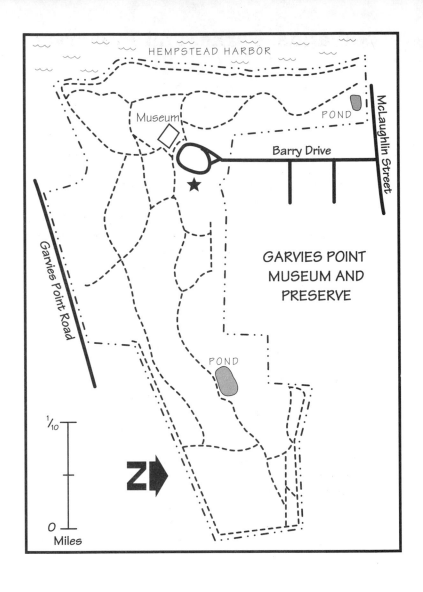

Garvies Point
Preserve and Museum

This sixty-two-acre area of glacial moraine has about 5 miles of marked nature trails over "the Carpenter Tract," purchased in 1668 from the Matinecock Indians. For thousands of years before this, woodland natives had hunted, gathered, and camped on this and adjoining lands. The concentrated remains of their middens here are one of the reasons Nassau County acquired the land in 1963 and opened the museum, which specializes in Native American archaeology as well as regional geology. Physically Garvies Point is similar in many ways to the Sands Point Preserve on the opposite side of Hempstead Harbor. It acquired the name from a former owner, Dr. Thomas Garvie, who emigrated from Scotland to Glen Cove in the early nineteenth century. The preserve is open daily 8:30 A.M. to dusk, but the museum is only open Tuesday through Saturday from 10:00 A.M. to 4:00 P.M., and Sunday from 1:00 to 4:00 P.M. Admission to the museum is $1.00 for adults and 50 cents for children.

A parking area adjoins the museum. Exhibits give you a fine introduction to Long Island before its discovery by Europeans. There is a sweeping view of Hempstead Harbor as you stand here at the museum, and the nature trails that start here provide good walking any time of year.

Although in the midst of suburban neighborhoods, the high ridge along the shore may set your mind to wondering about the state of the native people who stalked along it so many years ago. Those who greeted the settlers on Long Island were generally a congenial and helpful people and at first offered no resistance to the newcomers. Fish and game were plentiful, and they were adept at catching all that was needed. The northern climate here was ameliorated by the sea. Those early settlers recognized the advantages and were joined rather quickly by others who learned about the place. The history of these early days is well documented, and your local library may start you reading about these first encounters between the European settlers and the Native Americans.

During the warmer months, the preserve is full of wildlife; the woods and meadows attract a great variety of birds. Because there's an effort to keep it in a natural state, a wide variety of native plants grow here. You'll find forty-eight species of trees, including northern red oak, pin oak, sassafras, beech, black cherry, persimmon, tulip tree, locust, sycamore, and butternut hickory. It is all in all a very pleasant experience to roam over these unexpected riches.

If you walk along the seashore, you can inspect the rocky beach and the bluffs above it. The sand contains the glacial debris so characteristic of all the North Shore. Only a few spots on Long Island, however, have glacial deposits so unusually thin as they are here at Garvies Point, thus exposing 70-million-year-old deposits of sand, silts, and multicolored clays. Well-preserved fossils of Cretaceous plants have even been found along these shorefront cliffs.

From Long Island Expressway, Northern State Parkway, Northern Boulevard, or Meadowbrook Parkway, exit on Glen Cove Road, northbound. Continue on Glen Cove bypass (Route 107 North, keep left at fork) to last traffic light facing Glen Cove Fire House. Turn right and follow signs to the museum (571–8010).

18

Muttontown Preserve

Under the stewardship of the Nassau County Museum, this 550-acre preserve combines the assets of a number of old North Shore estates to provide a quiet, rural, and startlingly extensive area for woodland walks. Situated in East Norwich south of Route 25A and west of Route 106, it comprises four principal areas, two of which are of primary interest to walkers.

The first of these is the fifty-acre Nature Center area, which features a marked self-guiding trail running through an irregular U-shaped parcel that largely surrounds one of the old mansions, "Chelsea," which is now used for selected cultural exhibitions and affairs. The Bill Paterson Nature Center (571–8500) is at the end of Muttontown Lane, a little road running south off 25A in East Norwich. A parking area for the center and for walkers is in the preserve; the gate is open 9:30 A.M. to 4:30 P.M. daily. Behind the center is a little pond that was dug in 1967 to provide better drainage to the wet area here, and deciduous woods of swamp maple, pin oak, and tupelo, the tree closely related to the sourgum of southern swamps that turns scarlet in autumn. Although the pond doesn't support any fish, it does provide the environment needed by a variety of beetles and other insects and attracts turtles, frogs, and salamanders, as well as a variety of birds.

Happily the trails are marked with colored number posts, and this is most helpful to guide you along twisty, turny paths where otherwise you might miss seeing much the area offers.

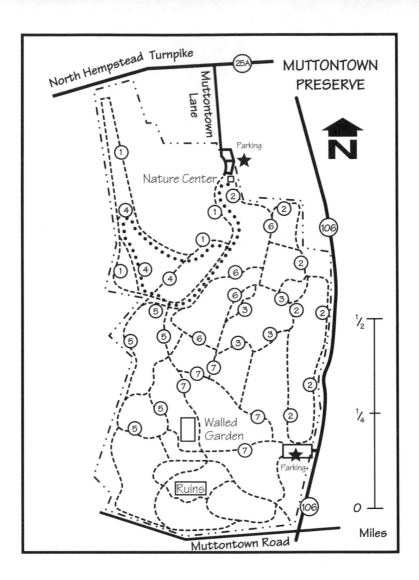

Many of the trees are marked, too, for identification. Watch out for poison ivy, which grows rankly throughout the preserve!

Follow the green markers for trail 1 through the swamp area where you will find arrowwood and spicebush growing, along with ferns, mosses, and liverworts, and you will come out on a large field, once farmland, now let go so that it attracts bobwhite and pheasant, field mice and red fox. Turn right here following the green blazes into the evergreen woods. On the hot summer day we walked here, the cool of these woods was noticeable. It is a forest of white pine and larch, with a scattering of dogwood and black cherry, and paths are spongy, so you stride forth with an easy gait.

Don't be upset if you lose your sense of direction. The path actually doubles back, and you find yourself turned around heading north on the green trail, which goes nearly back to Route 25A, before returning. Part way along you can cross over on the yellow marker (#4) if you prefer a shorter walk.

The other major area for walking is the contiguous 200-acre parcel south of the Nature Center trails down to Muttontown Road. The trails in this area are mainly bridle paths left over from the days when all this was horse country. They are mostly marked with colored and numbered posts as they wind through evergreen woods and open meadows, past glacially formed rolling hills and kettle-hole ponds. This section has its own parking area, entered from Route 106, about 1,000 feet north of the Muttontown Road intersection. This large lot is still actively used for horse trailers and supports both hikers and users of the equestrian practice areas.

This part of the preserve, along with 250 acres south of Muttontown Road that are not open for general use, comprised the Lansdell Christie estate. Some overgrown ruins in the woods north of Muttontown Road are the only remaining evidence of a mansion there that was once owned (but never used) by King Zog of Albania.

If everyone who walks here comes as a guest and is concerned and aware of the life preserved here, we shall have a treasured little sanctuary forever wild.

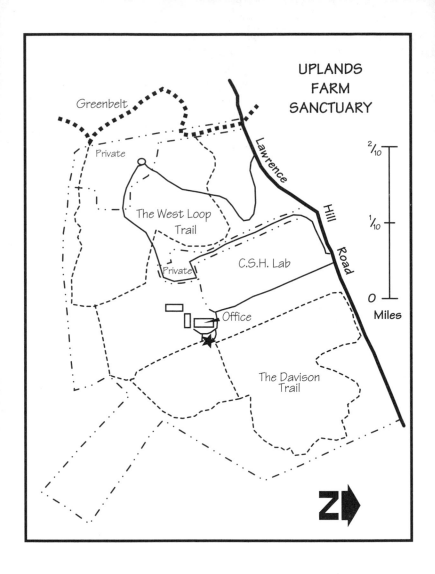

UPLANDS FARM SANCTUARY

Greenbelt

Private

The West Loop Trail

Private

Lawrence

Hill

Road

C.S.H. Lab

Office

The Davison Trail

$^2/_{10}$

$^1/_{10}$

0

Miles

Z

19

Uplands Farm Sanctuary

The Long Island Chapter of The Nature Conservancy (367–3225) has its headquarters in farm buildings that are surrounded by open fields and upland woods on Lawrence Hill Road, in Cold Spring Harbor, about a quarter mile east of the junction of Routes 25A and 108. There are trails through the preserve that not only visit varied terrain, but also connect with the Nassau-Suffolk Greenbelt Trail to permit a 2¼-mile loop walk. A detailed guide is available at the kiosk. The office is open weekdays 9:00 A.M. to 5:00 P.M., but the trails are open daily dawn to dusk.

We wrote briefly about The Nature Conservancy in the preface to this edition. Though it is a national organization, it works quietly and most effectively on the local level, and the two chapters on Long Island have been responsible for the acquisition of more than seventy natural areas here, many of them ecologically fragile. The Sunken Forest on Fire Island, the North Shore Wildlife Sanctuary, and a section of Caumsett State Park are all properties that The Nature Conservancy helped to set aside for conservation purposes.

We have walked a number of these natural areas that belong to the Conservancy with great satisfaction, and they are open to serious walkers with permits. If interested, you should contact the organization directly. With your help as a member, even more can be accomplished.

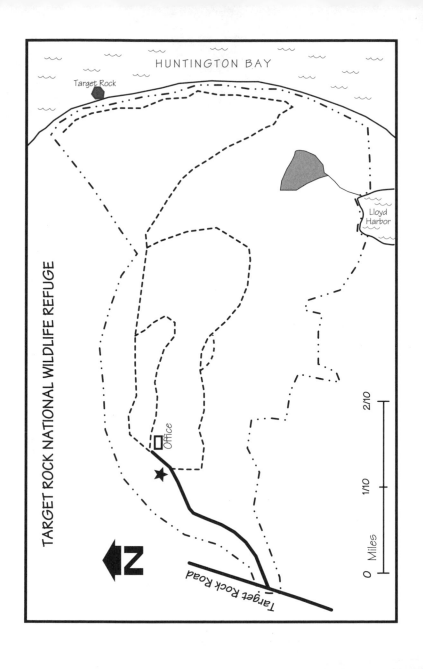

20

Target Rock
National Wildlife Refuge

This interesting refuge is, like the Elizabeth A. Morton National Wildlife Refuge, managed by the U.S. Fish and Wildlife Service to preserve endangered plants and animals, to preserve natural diversity, and to perpetuate migratory bird life. It covers eighty heavily wooded and rolling acres at the eastern end of Lloyd Neck and contains about 0.3 mile of beach on Huntington Bay south of Fort Point and Target Rock.

The refuge was once the estate of financier Ferdinand Eberstadt, who built a thirty-five-room neo-Georgian mansion there in 1937 on one of the higher points. After his death the property was deeded to the government in 1967 as a wildlife refuge. There is a half-mile trail to the beach that goes through mature oak-hickory woods and passes close to a brackish pond that always has a few waterfowl in residence. In addition, a new wheelchair-accessible trail leads from the beach trail at the office through the woods to the open field that was the site of the old mansion. There is also a quarter-mile side trail along the south side of the knob where the old mansion once sat. Along the trail is a grove of magnificent tall oaks.

The refuge is very popular with wildlife. All told, naturalists have identified more than 300 species of birds, mammals, reptiles, and amphibians in the Target Rock National Wildlife Refuge.

The trails are broad and easy to manage even as you stay on the lookout for wildlife; if you stay clear of grass at the beach, your risk of acquiring a tick should be minimal.

When you look north along the beach, you'll see two large boulders just offshore. They were once part of the glacial residue in the morainal bluff above them, but the land has eroded to the west to leave them in the bay. At the time of the American Revolution the bigger one was still up in the bank, but exposed, so British warships offshore used it as a gunnery target—hence the name Target Rock.

The refuge is open daily from 8:00 A.M. to dusk. It can be reached from Huntington by following West Neck Road and Lloyd Harbor Road 2.2 miles past the entrance to Caumsett State Park. Questions? Call 271–2409, or if no answer, call the Long Island National Wildlife Refuge complex at 286–0485.

There is a $4.00 entrance fee per car. Annual passes are available for $10.00, and Golden Age/Access Passports for seniors and the disabled are also honored.

21

Caleb Smith
State Park Preserve

This 543-acre tract dates back to 1663, when the first Smith bought the land from the Indians. Smith ownership continued for over 200 years until Caleb started selling parts of it to the Brooklyn Gun Club (later the Wyandanch Club). By 1900 the club had all the land and had completed their expansion of the original house to what you now see as the museum building. The property was bought by New York State in 1963 as part of a planned program of open space preservation. It is now open for "passive" recreation as an environmental preserve with ponds, a number of trails that total more than 5 miles (including the Long Island Greenbelt and two self-guiding nature trails), and a modest museum in the imposing old clubhouse.

Park hours are 8:00 A.M. to sunset; it's open Wednesday through Sunday all year, and also on Tuesday, April through September. There is a $4.00 vehicle fee every day from April 1 to Labor Day, and on weekends only from Labor Day to March 21 (265–1054). In case you plan to walk through the part of the preserve that is south of Route 25 or to pass through the whole preserve on the Greenbelt, be sure to get the combination for the locked gates you will encounter when you enter or leave the preserve, by phoning in advance or stopping at the museum.

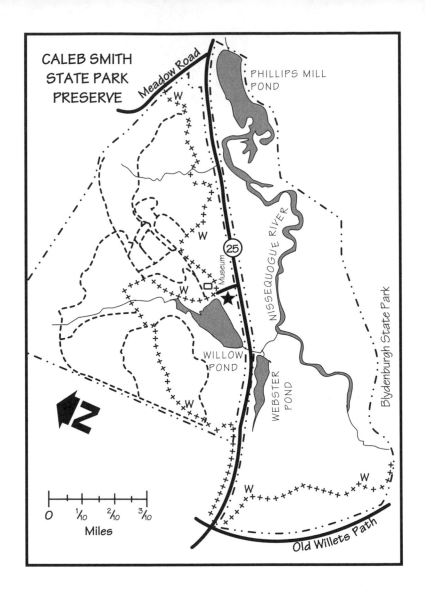

The preserve is bisected by Jericho Turnpike (Route 25), which runs in a curve southwesterly here. The entrance is off the northern side of the highway, 3 miles east of the Sagtikos State Parkway and .75 mile east of Old Willets Path. Be careful when turning into the parking area—this straightaway stretch of Route 25 encourages speeders!

One other survivor from colonial times (not open to the public) is the Aron Vail House, which was an inn on the old stage-coach route and a point of interest in early Smithtown history. On both sides of Route 25 the preserve is made up of swamp and upland and provides a fine habitat for many geese and ducks, a wide variety of birds, rabbits, raccoons, and native wildlife. We found the undulating trail soft and pleasant footing, remarkably quiet in one of the busiest sections of Suffolk County.

On our walk here we followed a number of trails blazed for cross-country skiing and stayed mostly on the northwest side of the preserve. These rolling slopes and hillsides are the northern side of the Ronkonkoma Moraine, and the drainage flows into the Nissequogue River, and into Long Island Sound.

The part of the preserve south of Route 25, where the Nissequogue meanders through ponds and lowlands, was a mecca for fly fishermen when it was a private club. It is now open to the public on a strict reservation basis and still provides excellent fly fishing.

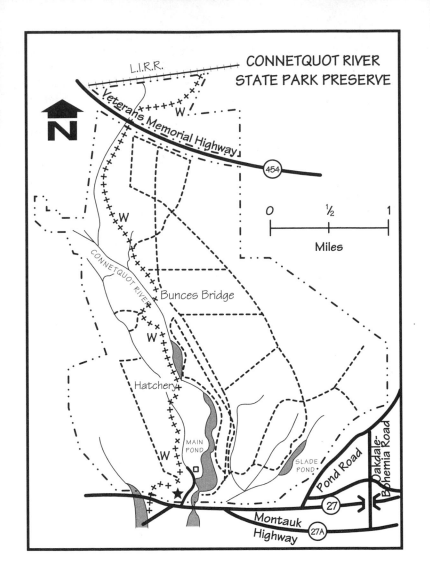

CONNETQUOT RIVER
STATE PARK PRESERVE

L.I.R.R.

Veterans Memorial Highway

N

W

454

0   ½   1

Miles

CONNETQUOT RIVER

Bunces Bridge

W

Hatchery

W

MAIN
POND

W

SLADE
POND

Pond Road

Oakdale-
Bohemia Road

27

Montauk
Highway

27A

22

Connetquot River
State Park Preserve

Connetquot River State Park Preserve is an ideal place to walk. It has a very special place in the Long Island State Park system; the designated term "preserve" means that there are no ball fields or playgrounds or picnic areas. The idea is to keep an area like this much as it has always been and to limit its use to "passive recreation," such as walking, horseback riding, and fishing. Bicycles are not permitted here.

In order to keep the character of the preserve undisturbed, walkers are required to get a permit in advance. Write to Connetquot River State Park, P.O. Box 505, Oakdale, NY 11769, giving name, address, and number of people in the party. The permit (good for a year) can be picked up at the gate when you arrive and pay the vehicle user fee of $4.00. The park is open year-round Wednesday through Sunday 8:00 A.M. to 4:30 P.M., and from April 1 through Labor Day it is also open Tuesday. If you have questions, call 581–1005.

A word about getting to its obscure entrance off the Sunrise Highway, Route 27, which is a divided three-lane highway that has been under major reconstruction. You can only enter Connetquot from the westbound lanes, so if you are headed east proceed past the park entrance about 1 mile to the Oakdale-Bohemia Road exit. Get off there, turn left over the bridge, and head west along the service road or right-hand lane to reach the park entrance. Look sharp for the white pavement markings of a very short exit lane.

An explanation of how an oasis this size, nearly 3,500 acres, is possible is in the deed, which was held by a syndicate of wealthy sportsmen as a private trout stream and hunting preserve for well over one hundred years. Before that, it was held as a patent dating back to pre-Revolutionary times. When you leave your car at the parking lot and stroll out by the buildings near the entrance booth, you will be seeing what was the clubhouse and what has been available to public access only since 1973. In days gone by, others who have walked these trails whom you just might have heard of include Daniel Webster, Ulysses S. Grant, General Sherman, Lorenzo Delmonico, and Charles L. Tiffany, to name a few—membership was limited to one hundred names at any time.

We headed out on the red blazed trail—there are miles and miles of trails, including a section of the north-to-south Long Island Greenbelt Trail—catching glimpses of the Connetquot River as we went along. It was late November, and all the migrating birds had passed through, but we saw hooded merganser, mallard, swan, and a female wood duck. We saw three deer, and surprised two rabbits, a squirrel, and a fox.

"It was a red fox. We have them here," Gil Bergen, the park superintendent who has managed the place for many years, told us. "You are lucky to see one in the daytime."

On a recent spring visit, our day was made complete by a close encounter with a couple of wild turkeys, the tom in gorgeous multicolor display and the hen trudging slowly along behind. It was an uncommon and beautiful sight.

23

Three Parks with Views

To suggest climbing hills on Long Island may appear frivolous, but since we have an urge to reach heights and see the view from there, it occurs to us that others may, too. That's why we're suggesting these three morainal hills that command unusual views for this area. West Hills County Park boasts Jayne's Hill, at 401.5 feet above sea level, the highest point on Long Island. Next comes Colonie Hill in Islip's Hidden Pond Park (180 feet), and then Bald Hill (285 feet) in Suffolk Hills County Park.

Jayne's Hill is in the northeast corner of West Hills Park, a heavily wooded area with an extensive network of blazed trails and woods roads that justify visiting it even without a view. The view is limited in width, but it is a fine outlook to the southwest, with the Atlantic, 13 miles away, easily seen on a clear day.

It's possible to drive nearly to the top of Jayne's Hill by finding Walt Whitman's old house off Route 110 in Melville (look for historic markers), and then going directly west from there (after a visit!) on West Hills Road, and then three blocks later turn left on Reservoir Road. This road rises steeply to end just below the top. Follow a footpath on the left side of the water tank to the high point and view.

If you'd like more exercise than this, then go to the park office for a free copy of a detailed trail map. The office is on High Hold Drive. You can get there from Jericho Turnpike (Route 25) by going south on Round Swamp Road 0.4 mile and turning left onto High Hold, or else try back roads west from Route 110. If

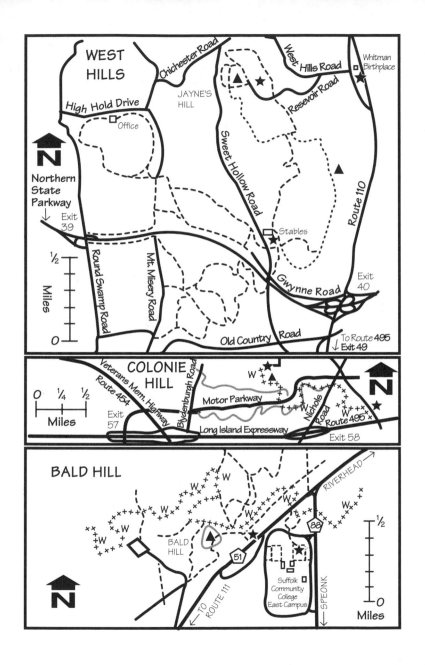

you then wish to explore the park or just hike up to Jayne's Hill, follow the map to reach Sweet Hollow Road and then go south on it to a parking and picnic area just beyond a big riding stable. By a variety of trails, Jayne's Hill is a bit more than a mile away.

The second lookout is Colonie Hill in Hauppage, where the Long Island Greenbelt Trail crosses the Ronkonkoma Moraine and passes through Hidden Pond Park. Here there are woodlands closely surrounded by "civilization," but the pleasant view north is won by a very short walk (under .25 mile) from where the trail crosses Motor Parkway. To get there go east on Motor Parkway from exit 57 of the Long Island Expressway (Route 495) to a point 1.2 miles beyond the intersection with Route 454. When you reach the point where some major high-tension lines cross overhead, stop and park. There is a gate in the north side fence there and a slim opening next to it where the white-blazed Greenbelt heads north. Follow it; when the trail turns west along the ridge line, you'll find the views, and a couple of benches to help you enjoy them. The bulk of the park is down below on the north side of the moraine; parking is available there, too.

The final lookout, Bald Hill, is about 3.5 miles south of Riverhead just off Route 51. It's in an undeveloped county park, but close to the highway, so it's easy to find. You have two choices here on ways to the top. If you want a quick and easy trip (climb 130 feet in 0.2 mile), park your car off the road by the gates, 0.6 mile south of where Routes 51 and 88 split. Go in past the barriers and follow the heavily worn road directly away from the highway. After about 600 feet there is a broad trail (jeep road) on your left heading nearly straight uphill. Take it, and in just a few minutes you'll be on top with a fine view northeast through a gap in the pines. Peconic Bay, Robins Island, and Shelter Island will all be visible on a good day. This whole venture should take about half an hour.

If instead you'd like to get an invigorating 2-mile walk in addition to the climb, go left on Route 88 when you reach it from Riverhead. After 0.3 mile, turn in at the entrance to Suffolk Community College and go right into the big east parking field and head for the northwest corner, where there is a fine, roofed map and notice board. Park there and follow a clear but poorly maintained yellow-blazed nature trail roughly north to and along the west edge of a big glacial kettle hole. At a junction with the white-blazed Pine Barrens Trail (Paumanok Path), go left on it, cross Route 51, and follow the trail southwest, parallel to Route 51, until you come to an area of heavily torn-up woods roads. There you will easily find the short way up the northeast face of Bald Hill. An alternative route from that area is to follow other trails around the right (west) face of the knob until you find one that goes basically due east as it makes a more gradual climb to the top. This route means a 3-mile round-trip from your car, with a fair amount of up and down as well.

You'll find many roads leading off into these woods. Extend your walks and enjoy them while you can, but don't get lost—it's easy to do in the Pine Barrens. In fact, if you're serious about exploring this area, we suggest you contact the Long Island Greenbelt Trail Conference (see p. xii) to get a copy of their Long Island Pine Barrens Trail map or any other current offerings. U.S. Geological Survey maps are good, too, but are not nearly as complete or up to date with trail information,

24

Wertheim National Wildlife Refuge

Long Island has nine National Wildlife Refuges, one of which (Target Rock) we have already covered. They all share the common goal of providing habitat for migratory and resident birds and for other indigenous wildlife. With the exception of Jamaica Bay, which is administered separately, they have common management by the Long Island National Wildlife Refuge Complex, centered at the Wertheim Refuge in Shirley (286–0485).

Wertheim is notable both for size (2,400 acres) and for the diversity of habitats it provides. About half are aquatic and half are uplands. A prominent feature is the Carmans River, the second-longest river on Long Island. Together with Bellport Bay, they are the keys to water-based life, since they vary in salinity from fresh to brackish to almost fully saline in the bay. Both are complemented by extensive marshes, swamps, and marine grasslands. The upland areas are on a sandy glacial outwash plain, with pitch pine, oak-pine, and oak-red maple stands being dominant.

Diverse habitats lead to diverse inhabitants; at the Wertheim Refuge these include over 240 species of birds. A high proportion of the birds are migratory, and Wertheim is a favored stop on the Atlantic flyway. Visitors will enjoy the excellent nature trail that

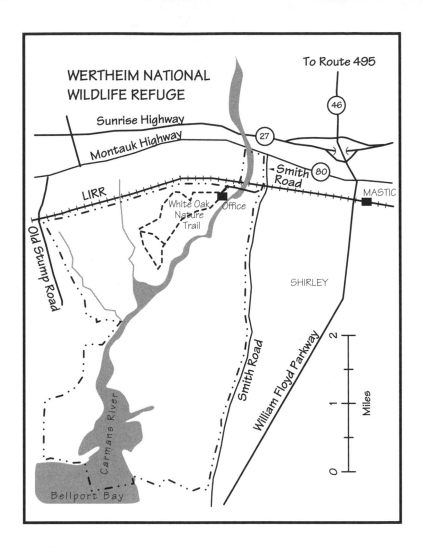

covers 3 miles in a big loop starting at the refuge office, with a shortcut available in the middle that makes for a 1.5-mile loop. This White Oak Nature Trail has two blinds for viewing open field areas and waterways. Visitors are effectively hidden from being noticed by the birds and animals out in the open, yet have an unimpeded view of them.

The best seasons for viewing are difficult to define because of the great variety of species here. Migratory waterfowl are present in the greatest numbers from October through April. Resident birds are most active during the day, as are the deer and wild turkey, but the smaller animals favor dawn and dusk when the refuge may not be open. You can't really expect to have a lot of sightings in any one visit, but repeated visits should pay off. Trying different seasons and times should provide a good representation of Long Island's native flora and fauna.

The refuge is located on the south shore of Long Island about 6 miles east of Patchogue. From the Long Island Expressway (Route 495, exit 68) go south on William Floyd Parkway (Route 46) about 3 miles to the intersection directly *after* the exit from Sunrise Highway. This is Montauk Highway (Route 80). Turn right on it. Go about 1.5 miles and then turn left at the traffic light. Head south on Smith Road for about ⅛ mile (just after the railroad tracks) to the refuge entrance on the right. Follow the entrance road about .05 mile to the visitor parking area and information kiosk. Visiting hours are Monday through Friday 8:00 A.M. to 4:30 P.M. All visitors are asked to sign in at the kiosk. An excellent brochure is available there for the nature trail. For more information, stop in the adjacent office building or call 286–0485.

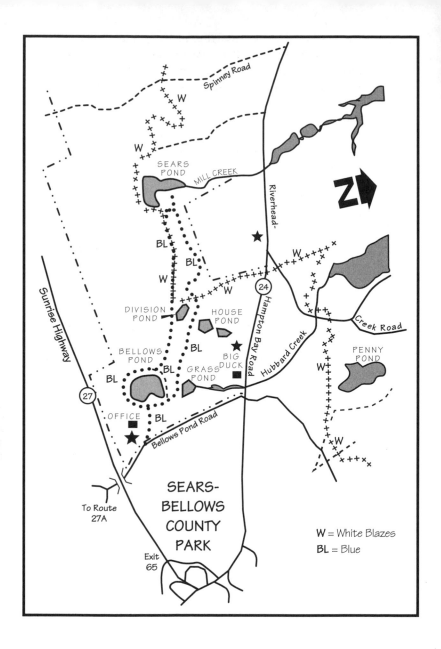

25

Sears-Bellows County Park

Sears-Bellows lies to the north of the Sunrise Highway (Route 27) and south of Flanders Road (Route 24), but fortunately has enough acreage to offer a feeling of remoteness, complete with two lakes, some ponds, and lots of cover for deer and game birds, including the marvelously colored wood duck. Walking here is most pleasant in spring or fall, but people are essentially gregarious, we have observed, and like to be where the crowd is, enjoying the fishing and boating at the big lake, Bellows. Thus, even when we walk here in season, in a few easy strides away from the camping area you lose almost everyone.

You will find parking spaces here, as in all Suffolk County parks, limited in season to Suffolk County residents with permits. Trails are not heavy traffic areas, and hikers are not discouraged, so if you do not have the permit, the park staff will usually treat you courteously if you are not a nuisance.

The park is open daily all year but may have shorter daily hours off-season. An additional concern is that some areas in the park are open to hunting in mid-winter, so before heading off into the woods in the November-through-January period, check with the park office (852–8290) for any restrictions or for park hours.

The best entry to the park is on Bellows Pond Road off the Flanders Road (Route 24), 5 miles south of the Riverhead traffic circle and 1.8 miles from exit 65 on Route 27.

Many dirt roads make good paths through the woodlands and around the lakes, and if it is a quiet day when you come, the walk around Bellows Pond is an easy one. Our favorite walk, however, is from Bellows to Sears Pond. The paths are especially nice for walking, pine needles underfoot, mostly wide, and unobstructed. Go south of Bellows Pond first, then on the west side take a sharp left onto the newly defined Sears Pond trail, whose blue blazes lead quite directly from the park entrance area to the pond. You will pass through the woods, where we always seem to flush out a grouse or two, past a pond on the right that is a favorite haunt of the wood duck, then swing to the left and into a clearing that has a significant rise of land on it. We usually climb the rise and sit for a few minutes because there often is a red-tailed hawk here circling, and there is a view of the surrounding country. We continue on the path on the other side of the hill and walk about a mile northwestward through sparse, burned-over woods. The growth and vegetation increases heavily as you come to Sears Pond. Go down to the water quietly; the ducks are wary in this secluded hideaway.

You should note that a few trails on the west side of the park have been set aside for the exclusive use of horse riders and are closed to hikers and not shown on this map. While we hate to lose trails. this has to be a good move where dual use is heavy.

Although it is quiet enough to listen to the birdsong and hear the flapping of the duck's wing, the muffled traffic noises from the two highways do carry across the treetops, as do jet sounds of overhead planes on their route to New York and punctuations from monstrous earth-moving equipment or chain saws. This is true, of course, anyplace on Long Island, and Sears-Bellows is as free today of the sounds of our civilization as almost anywhere else. So we can be grateful for the relative calm and tranquility and hope that others, too, will recognize it and strive to perpetuate it. And be thankful for the settings provided for public use by a foresighted Suffolk County Park Commission.

26

Mashomack Preserve

Mashomack is unique. In its 2,000 acres of woodlands, marshes, and tidal creeks it provides a greater variety of habitats and a greater variety of birds than any other area in Long Island. It occupies the southeastern third of Shelter Island, between the twin forks, and so can only be reached by a short ferry ride (South Ferry is closer and quicker than North Ferry). We are able to enjoy it only because it was purchased in 1980 by The Nature Conservancy from a far-seeing family.

The feature most notable, other than the tremendous scenic beauty of the preserve, is its vastness. Walking on some of the 17 miles of trails here, it's hard to believe you are only 90 miles from New York City. At Mashomack, together with protected areas to the south around Northwest Harbor, a maritime environment of unsurpassed richness has been given a fighting chance. The area's extensive salt marshes are vitally significant as a breeding ground and nursery for organisms at the bottom of the food chain, upon which all other life depends.

Four well-marked trails offer hikes of varying lengths and difficulty, up to 11 miles. All of them start at the Visitor Center, in the entrance area. On weekends volunteer naturalists can answer questions about natural history and the archaeology of the preserve. The gift shop is soon to be joined by a teaching center overlooking a kettle hole. There is also a trail for the handicapped

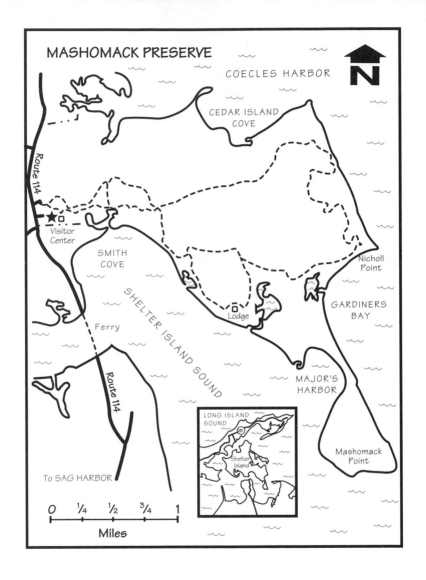

and visually impaired, featuring a wide variety of native plants.

Mashomack can easily be reached from either north or south as Route 114 connects both ferries. The preserve entrance is on the east side of the road, 0.9 mile from the South Ferry. The Visitor Center is but a short walk from the parking area. It and the preserve are open daily, from dawn to dusk, from May to September, and on weekends year-round, with a suggested donation of $1.50 for adults. For further information call 749–1001.

The majority of the preserve is upland oak and beech forest, which includes a rare pine swamp complex, the only community of its kind known to occur on Long Island. There is almost no open water in this wetland, and all of the plants are rooted in a floating mat of sphagnum moss. Because of its ability to retain many times its own weight in water, sphagnum moss plays an important part in keeping wetlands moist during dry periods.

An abundance of bird life makes Mashomack a paradise for ornithologists. As many as eighty-two breeding species have been recorded, and fifty-six different species winter at the preserve. To truly appreciate Mashomack, it is important to visit during all of the seasons and at different times of the day. Spring is marked by the return of the first pairs of ospreys from South America. More than any other creature, they represent the wild spirit of Mashomack. They can be seen all along the shores plunging down for fish and circling triumphantly with their catch. Summer is when most visitors come, and an early morning walk will be filled with birdsong in the upland areas.

In the autumn, hundreds of black ducks, Canada geese, and other migrating birds stop over at Mashomack. This is one of the best times for bird-watching, as the fall foliage provides a backdrop of exploding colors; the scarlet of red maple and sweet gum, golden beech leaves, red dogwoods, and orange bittersweet.

Winter offers an excellent opportunity for tracking deer, fox, raccoon, and even mink, which leave their signatures in the snow. The more adventurous can follow the trail along Gardiners Bay and catch a glimpse of harbor seals basking on rocks in the winter sun.

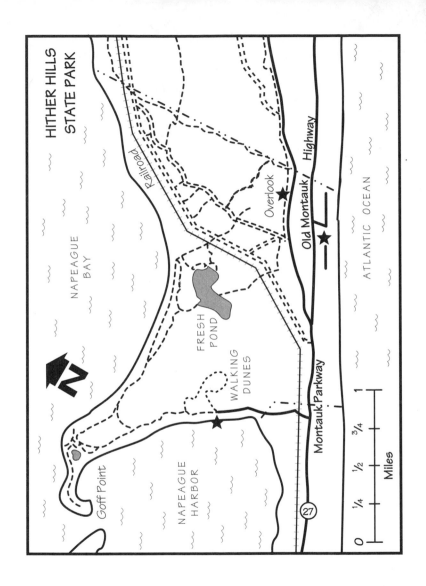

27

Hither Hills State Park

The Hither Hills area contains a 1,755-acre state park and two preserves totaling 1,340 acres. They come at the east end of the long, narrow finger of land that connects the prehistoric Montauk Island with the South Fork at Amagansett. The state park includes the long, sandy triangle that is the eastern shore of Napeague Harbor, the western half of the morainal upland, and about 1.3 miles of ocean and campground to the south. The balance of the upland, extending a bit over 2 miles along the north side of Montauk Parkway (Route 27), contains two contiguous preserves. The whole area has many sand roads and trails in the mixed pine-oak forest, and natural features and wildlife that make it attractive to the walker. There is too much to see in one day, so you should plan ahead and come armed with maps and data to make your visit more rewarding.

When you first arrive here, make a point of stopping for a few minutes at the overlook on Route 27, on your left as you reach the highest level of the moraine (the second crest). Leave your car to survey the panorama and get oriented. In the foreground you'll find a grassy area with a few trees that was decimated in a 1986 forest fire, and is now recovered but not quite a forest yet. Beyond it you have a good view of Napeague Harbor, with the Atlantic on the left, and the southwest end of Block Island Sound and Gardiners Island to the right. This is also a good central place to park while you explore the park and preserves (no parking along Route 27, technically a parkway).

The western triangle has the harbor shore on the west, a long beach facing Block Island Sound on the north, and wooded uplands on the east. There are two areas to visit here that you will enjoy. The first is the Walking Dunes, an interesting group of sand hills that are very gradually creeping across the flat terrain in response to prevailing northwest winds. As they move they gradually cover the trees in their path, while the trees respond by growing taller. It's probably a draw most of the time. The advancing face of the dunes is beautifully rounded and smooth, while there's a nice view from the dune crest. To find the dunes, look for a gated railroad grade crossing at the east end of the long, straight stretch on Route 27 from Amagansett, just before the hills begin. Take the paved road over the crossing and proceed straight north to the end of the pavement, about .75 mile. Park on the side of the road where there is an information kiosk at the start of the nature trail. Get a Walking Dunes leaflet and set off east on the trail. You'll be on the side of a steep dune in only a few hundred feet. Ill-defined paths through the trees and underbrush to the right will enable you to climb up the side without too much fuss, but do avoid disturbing the advancing face of the dunes.

The route to Goff Point is obvious along the harbor shore, but for an easier path, follow the shore for only a few hundred yards beyond the pavement until there's a gap in the sand bank on the right. Go through the gap and you will soon find a firm interior sand road that makes for easy walking either to the point or to the northern shore.

Another nice place to visit is Fresh Pond, a favorite with fishermen, birds, and other animals. Probably the best route to the pond is by the trails and roads from the overlook. Use the East Hampton Trails map (see p. 92 for more information) as your guide, and you should have little trouble.

The two preserves that lie to the east of the state park begin where the power lines head northeast and downhill from Route

27, a short distance east of the overlook. They offer several miles of woods roads, easy trails, and bayside bluffs. To visit these preserves the best place to park is at the entrance to the town recycling center, 2 miles east of the overlook on Route 27. Park just off the highway close to, but not in front of, the barred road on the left that leads to the interior.

Your enjoyment of the Hither Hills area will be greatly enhanced if, before you arrive there, you buy two very useful items. One is an excellent Hither Hills trail map that you can get from the town clerk at the East Hampton town offices, at 159 Pantigo Road (Route 27). It is the key to not getting lost in the woods! The other is the *South Fork–Shelter Island Preserve Guide* issued by The Nature Conservancy, P.O. Box 5125, East Hampton, NY 11937. It's an excellent 75-page booklet that tells you a great deal about 28 preserves in the South Fork areas east of Southampton. It has details on how to find each preserve, trail directions, and what is interesting about each from a naturalist's viewpoint.

The park and preserves are open daily, without charge, all year. You should know, however, that hunting is permitted at various times in the park during the late fall and winter. We suggest you call the park office at 668–2461 or 668–5000 to find out the exact dates of the open seasons for various types of game. Another good source of information is the New York State Department of Environmental Conservation in Stony Brook (444–0273), which issues the necessary hiking permits.

Former Estates

In the era beginning about 1900 and extending through the twenties, literally hundreds of wealthy people bought tracts of land on Long Island to create estates for themselves. The favored areas were along the shores of the sound and in the gentle hills of Nassau and western Suffolk, north of main arteries like Jericho Turnpike and the railroad. It is estimated that at least 500 major properties were acquired and mansions built on this Gold Coast, surely a unique suburban concentration.

Today, however, it is a different story. Population pressure and financial problems have resulted in most of the estates being broken up, mansions being demolished, and more modest homes being built (many still costing in the millions) in the spaces thus freed. A few of the big houses were acquired by schools, colleges, religious institutions, and various other public groups. In some cases the land remains undisturbed but the mansion has vanished, as you will note from some of the walks in this section. In others, the mansion remains essentially unchanged and competes with the landscaped grounds for your attention.

This pattern of dividing and altering estates holds for all but one, Blydenburgh. It had remained, until 1938, under the ownership of a single family since Colonial times. As a result the house is not grand, but it has a fine setting overlooking the pond and mill that brought the owners their prosperity.

If you are intrigued by these estates, as we were, you might like to visit your library to read an elegant volume by Monica Randall entitled *Mansions of Long Island's Gold Coast.* It has descriptions and photographs of a generous cross section of these estates, of their owners, and of their fates. It's a fascinating book.

Phipps Mansion, Old Westbury Gardens

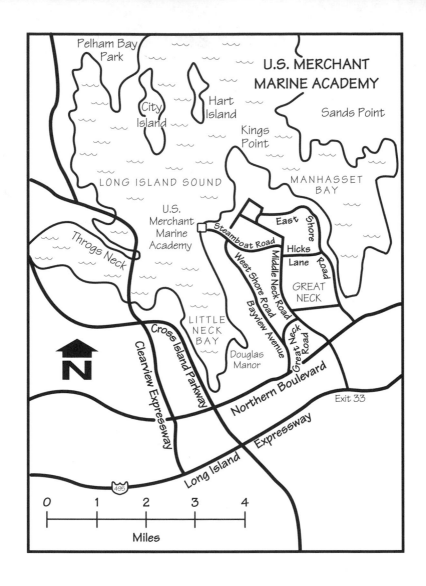

28

U.S. Merchant Marine Academy

Although fenced and entered through a guarded gate, the U.S. Merchant Marine Academy in Kings Point is open to the public daily from 8:00 A.M. to 4:30 P.M., and the eighty-two-acre grounds, formerly the estate of automobile magnate Walter P. Chrysler, make for a pleasant visit. The young American men and women who have the good fortune to get their education at this beautiful place should count themselves lucky in many ways. They have a stunning 180-degree view of Long Island Sound—the daintily soaring spans of the Throgs Neck and Whitestone Bridges and the cubes and rectangles of Manhattan. The campus includes docks with an impressive variety of boats used by officers-in-training to gain the experience necessary to handle any kind of vessel.

There are three buildings that deserve a visit, all on the bluff overlooking the sound and waterfront. To the south is the handsome Memorial Chapel; near it the white administrative center (Wiley Hall), the home of Walter P. Chrysler for many years; and at the north end the American Merchant Marine Museum. It features a history of the academy, an exceptionally fine collection of more than fifty ship models, and other memorabilia. The curator is Frank Braynard, the noted marine author, artist, and lecturer. The museum (773–5515) is open Tuesday through Friday, 10:00 A.M. to 3:00 P.M. and Saturday and Sunday 1:00 to 4:30 P.M., but it is closed from the last weekend of June to the first weekend of August and on federal holidays.

The academy is located on Steamboat Road, facing Long Island Sound, and a circuit of the campus makes an interesting, easy walk. If they appeal to you, you may watch regimental reviews some Saturday mornings in the spring and fall (773–5000).

As for the training here, it is 100 percent science and engineering. The graduate achieves a bachelor of science degree, a U.S. Coast Guard license as a third mate or a third assistant engineer, and a commission as ensign in the U.S. Naval Reserve. There is no tuition. The ages of the students range from seventeen to twenty-five. The daily routine begins at 6:10 A.M., with classes from 8:00 A.M. to noon and 1:30 to 5:00 P.M.; lights off at 11:00 P.M. The school offers independent study and sea training on board merchant vessels. Two graduates from the class of 1942 who chose other careers after spending their early years at sea are J. Lane Kirkland, former president of the AFL-CIO, and Dr. Thomas Nicholson, who became director of the American Museum of Natural History.

29

Sands Point Preserve

Comprising 216 acres of prime Long Island real estate, Sands Point Preserve stands on splendid bluffs overlooking Long Island Sound at the mouth of Hempstead Harbor, just north of Port Washington. For walkers it has six short, blazed trails and a small pond on land that supports a surprisingly wide range of plants and bird life. There is a mile of beachfront to explore as well. It is said that geologists find much of interest along here, in case you have rock-hounding tendencies. In the wooded areas there are native trees that were here when the first settlers arrived and also specimen oriental varieties that were brought in at the turn of the century.

No doubt these acres were groomed and manicured when the Goulds and then the Guggenheims lived here, but they are wilder now. There are two old manor houses and a large structure built to resemble a castle, Ireland's Kilkenny Castle in fact, but to serve as a stable. Today this building houses special traveling exhibits on natural history, the visitor center, and the museum shop.

The two mansions, one (Hempstead House) built by the Gould family, were subsequently owned by the Guggenheims. Harry Guggenheim, who was an early flying enthusiast and admirer of the young Charles A. Lindbergh, built the other (Falaise) in 1923. Harry's home was the scene of many gracious social

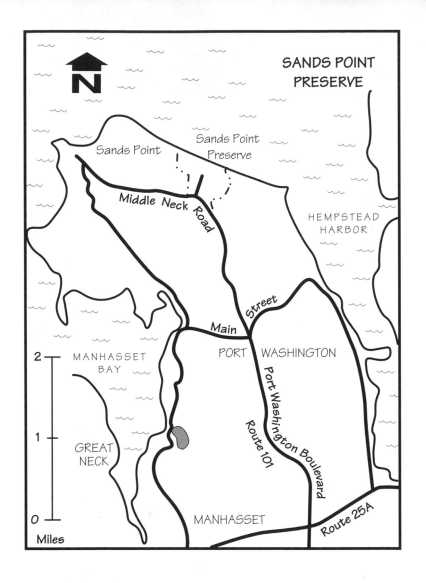

gatherings, for he was an outgoing man with many influential friends. When Lindbergh completed his historic flight across the Atlantic and returned to America, he was hard-pressed to find any escape from the mobs who awaited him everywhere he went. Harry Guggenheim gave him sanctuary at Falaise. The strong friendship that developed between these two, the worldly and sophisticated older man and the inexperienced, shy young flier, is a remarkable story, too long to tell here.

Since Sands Point is an easy commute to New York and yet presents the aura of gracious country living together with access to the water and fine water views, the private homes out here tend to be large, protectively landscaped, and expensive. So it is indeed a privilege to have this fine old estate open to the public.

Since Falaise can only be seen on an escorted tour, you'll need to plan ahead. It is a comfortable and cozy Norman French country house, well worth a visit, and it shows the owners' gracious lifestyle. Conducted hourly, tours require reservations and cost an extra $4.00 beyond the admission fee to the preserve ($1.00 weekends only in July and August). They're conducted in the afternoons; children under twelve are not permitted.

Hempstead House is also an exhibit building, featuring more than 2,000 pieces of Wedgewood ceramics (the Buten Collection), with a $1.00 fee.

The preserve is managed by the Nassau County Department of Recreation and Parks. Because of financial belt-tightening, its museum is not normally open in the winter, though the grounds remain open without charge. In general, the museum season runs from February through October, with some special exhibits scheduled at other times during the year. There are usually extra fees for the special exhibits. Daily hours are from 10:00 A.M. to 5:00 P.M.; closed Monday. For information on current events, specific museum/exhibit hours, and for Falaise tour reservations (afternoons only), call 571–7900.

Of course, if antiques leave you cold, the trails and grounds alone should justify a visit. Stop at the visitor center for a trail map, and enjoy nature.

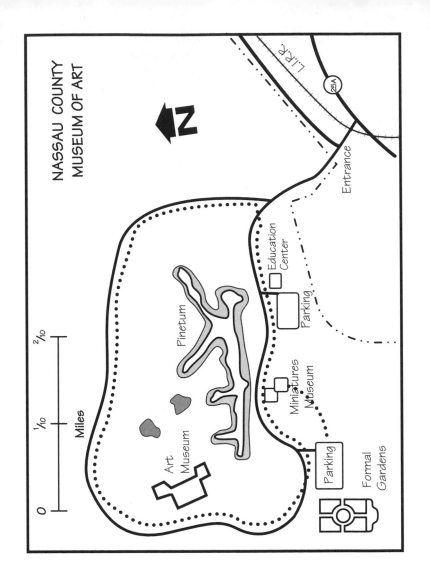

NASSAU COUNTY
MUSEUM OF ART

N

Miles

0   ¹⁄₁₀   ²⁄₁₀

Art
Museum

Pinetum

Education
Center

Parking

Miniatures
Museum

Parking

Formal
Gardens

Entrance

25A

L.I.R.R.

30

Nassau County Museum of Art

It wouldn't surprise us if William Cullen Bryant had been sitting on the very site of today's Nassau County Museum of Art when he wrote:

> *To him who, in the love of Nature, holds*
> *Communion with her visible forms, she speaks*
> *A various language.*

This was once his farmland, and he loved wandering over it. Today, nature's visible forms still show themselves in nice variety, and a walk here is a quieting experience, even though it lies just off the busy thoroughfare of Northern Boulevard.

The Nassau County Museum of Art now occupies an imposing Georgian mansion on the hilltop that was last owned by the son of Henry Clay Frick, a co-founder of U.S. Steel. He lived there for nearly fifty years and did much to improve the main building and the surrounding 145 acres of woodland and meadow. He had an active interest in nature, kept a variety of animals and birds, and planted a fine pinetum that still survives today. The property was bought by Nassau County after his death in 1965, and the main house was converted to its present use after that.

The museum is well worth visiting to see the changing special exhibitions, which are the primary attractions. Predominantly keyed to modern art, they offer interesting views into many facets of the art world. It is good to phone before visiting, since the museum proper is usually closed for brief periods while a new exhibit is hung. The grounds, of course, are always open, and the best introduction to them is by first walking the perimeter road (a 1-mile loop) to get the lay of the land. Then explore the open fields and informal paths through the woods. There are no marked trails, but you should visit the pinetum as well as the formal garden next to the parking lot. On the northwest side of the grounds you may spot a striking Gothic Revival cottage that Bryant had built in 1862 (now being restored).

One striking feature of the area is the presence of more than thirty modern sculptures in natural settings throughout the grounds. Some were commissioned, others are on extended loan, but all provide an interesting contrast to the parklike background. Be sure to get a "sculpture map" at the museum to guide you.

Just east of the parking lot you will find the new Tee Ridder Miniatures Museum. This fascinating exhibit includes 26 miniature rooms, a Neoclassical doll house, and other exhibits of miniature art.

Do walk through the pinetum. It is more than just a shady place to stroll. In its heyday under Mr. Frick, it had more than 190 species of conifers, making it one of the best collections in America. Today it is mature and less exceptional, but it is still interesting and instructive to walk down the central corridor to see the seven species groups (firs, pines, hemlocks, spruces, yews, cypresses, and cedars). A leaflet with more details should be available at the museum.

The museum entrance is clearly marked on Northern Boulevard (just east of the railroad overpass at the top of the rise from the Roslyn Village area), and there is ample free parking. It is open Tuesday through Sunday from 11:00 A.M. to 5:00 P.M., and admission to both museums is $4.00 for adults, less for seniors and students. There is a pleasant small cafe in one wing, though you might be tempted to bring a sandwich to enjoy on a hillside near the woods. Museum information? Call 484–9338.

31

Old Westbury Gardens

Long Island is fortunate in that of the 500 estates that were built on the north shore Gold Coast between 1900 and 1925, two of the very best remain for us to enjoy—Old Westbury Gardens and Planting Fields Arboretum. Both have gracious mansions, and both have superb landscapes and gardens that we can envy and perhaps copy (in parts). Both are large enough in area and diverse enough in their features to permit strolling about, endlessly finding new aspects to admire.

On balance, we're inclined to prefer Old Westbury. While smaller in extent, it has magnificent allées, several ponds, and a bevy of gardens that are a tribute to the taste of Londoner George Crawley, the designer for both the mansion and grounds. Planting Fields has naturally rolling terrain, plantings of trees and shrubs that are extensive and varied enough to warrant the *arboretum* label, and of course the famous greenhouses. We'll speak of it next.

Old Westbury Gardens can be reached from the Long Island Expressway by leaving it at exit 39 south, taking the service road east 1.2 miles to Old Westbury Road, and then turning right on it to reach the entrance in ¼ mile. It is open Wednesday through Monday from 10:00 A.M. to 5:00 P.M. from late April through October, and also in December for special holiday events in the mansion. There is a $6.00 admission fee to the grounds and a

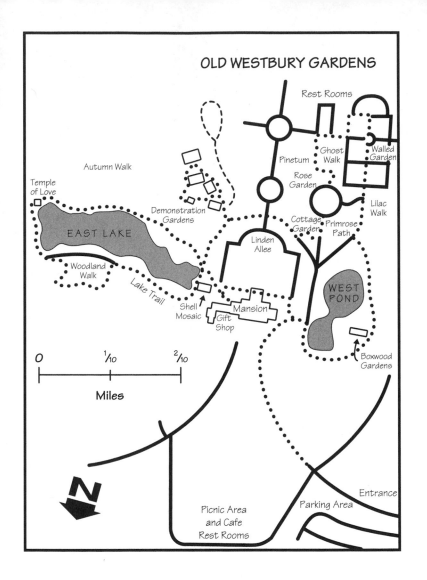

OLD WESTBURY GARDENS

Rest Rooms

Autumn Walk

Pinetum

Ghost Walk

Walled Garden

Rose Garden

Temple of Love

EAST LAKE

Demonstration Gardens

Lilac Walk

Cottage Garden

Primrose Path

Linden Allee

Woodland Walk

Lake Trail

WEST POND

Shell Mosaic

Mansion

Gift Shop

Boxwood Gardens

0   1/10   2/10

Miles

N

Picnic Area and Cafe Rest Rooms

Parking Area

Entrance

separate $4.00 fee for the mansion tour. For information on the many special events, call 333–0048.

You enter through wrought-iron gates and a towering allée of linden trees. The grass is tended, and grand allées and hedges of beeches, hemlocks, and linden stretch a half mile to the north and south of the mansion. After parking you start to encounter the many surprises of the landscape by embarking on a 1.3-mile self-guided tour that could take up to two hours. You are gently steered to the boxwood garden, Italianate two-acre walled garden, pinetum, rose garden, Ghost Walk, cottage garden, demonstration garden, woodland walk, and more. You return to the stately seventeenth-century, Charles II–style country house after this vista of gracious living that John S. Phipps and his family enjoyed and encounter the indoor counterpart of their gardens.

When you come into the house, there are fresh flowers in all rooms, and the dinner table is set; it is just as though the Phipps family had stepped out but would be back shortly, as though you were an invited weekend guest. The rooms are pleasant—light, airy, homey, and tastefully decorated by someone with a fine sense of color. Although the home is not ostentatious, it displays evidence of considerable wealth—English antiques; paintings by Reynolds, Raeburn, Gainsborough, Constable, and Sargent; gilded mirrors and crystal chandeliers.

To further the ambiance, there is a nice picnic area in the woods with a self-service "Café in the Woods" for light refreshments. All in all, it's a place to visit again and again, ever fresh and ever lovely.

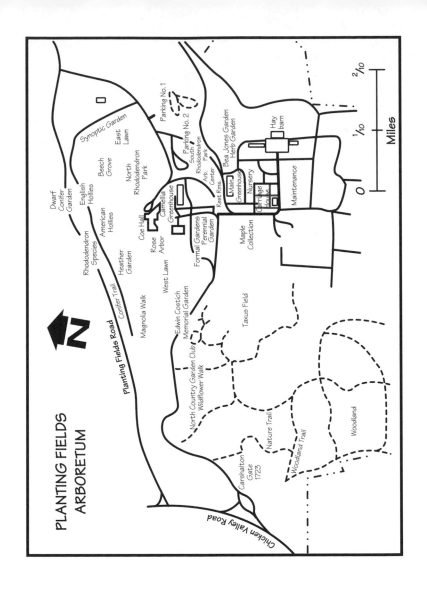

32

Planting Fields Arboretum

Planting Fields Arboretum State Historic Park is one of the best loved places on Long Island's Gold Coast, probably because it appeals to so many interests. The 409 acres of woodlands, rolling lawns and fields, and cultivated gardens provide a wonderful setting for the Tudor-Revival mansion Coe Hall and for a flock of greenhouses and other buildings.

In truth, the mansion and the landscaping compete as equals for the visitor's applause as the most noteworthy sights, thanks to the vision of William Robertson Coe. He bought the lands and the first house on the estate in 1913, and in 1918 began to build the present sixty-five-room mansion in a style of architecture reflecting what was popular during the reign of Queen Elizabeth I. Outstanding craftsmanship and meticulous detailing can be seen in hand-carved chimneys, stonework, and woodwork. The period rooms are fully restored and reflect an age of grace and luxury. Guided tours are available daily in the afternoons April through October, for a $3.50 fee. There are occasional special events to disturb normal schedules—you can check by calling 922–9200.

For the walker, landscaping rises to the fore. Designed by Frederick Law Olmsted Jr. in the early 1920s, the arboretum offers a spectacular display of trees and shrubs, many imported from abroad. The sweeping lawns boast majestic beech and linden trees, as well as cedar, fir, elm, tulip, maple, holly, oak, and magnolia. Beyond the lawns are native fields and forest, with laurel, rhododendron, and dogwood much in evidence along the drives and trails.

In contrast to the lawns are specialized garden areas and shrub plantings, including rose, dwarf conifer, rhododendron, and synoptic gardens, and extensive annual, perennial, and bulb plantings. Then there is the magnificent Camellia Greenhouse to visit for late-winter beauty and the Main Greenhouse for specialized collections and seasonal displays.

There are many different ways to enjoy Planting Fields, and the simple one of wandering at will across the lawns, through the gardens, and along woodland paths and drives surely makes up for the lack of a specific route or trail for the walker to follow. Practically every area and season has something to offer.

Planting Fields is managed by the New York State Department of Parks and is open every day of the year (except Christmas) from 9:00 A.M. to 5:00 P.M. The greenhouses are open from 10:00 A.M. to 4:00 P.M., and a call to 922–9200 will let you discover what special exhibitions are in progress. Admission to the grounds is $4.00 per car all year on weekends and holidays and also on weekdays between May 1 and Labor Day. Weekdays off-season are free. To reach Planting Fields, turn north off Route 25A, on Wolver Hollow Road, following it until it ends at Chicken Valley Road. Turn right and follow Chicken Valley Road for just over 2 miles and then turn right (shortly after you pass some magnificent English wrought-iron gates) on Planting Fields Road to the entrance.

33

Caumsett State Park

Since 1961, 1,500 acres of the original 1,750-acre estate overlooking Long Island Sound, which made up the fabulous English-style domain of Marshall Field III, has been owned by New York State. Today it is administered by the Long Island State Park and Recreation Commission, and is a grand place to walk.

A grand place in every way because there are not apt to be crowds, with the many restrictions—no picnicking facilities (so you must pack your sandwich, bring your own drinking water, carry away your leftovers), no swimming, no pets, no playgrounds, no camping, and no driving beyond the parking area at the park booth, a matter of 2 miles to Long Island Sound.

This gives Caumsett a wonderfully remote aspect once you walk beyond the marvelous old farm buildings and magnificent stable nearby or down along the shore, so plan to spend the better part of a day. It is open Memorial Day through Labor Day from 8:00 A.M. to 4:30 P.M. daily. The entrance fee is $4.00. To get there from Route 25A in Huntington, turn north on West Neck Road to the park, a very pretty 5.5 miles.

It is hard to imagine that one man owned this vast park and that it was a farm that made its own power and was self-sufficient in most every way. Miles of roads were built for motoring and horseback riding. There was tennis, indoors and out, pheasant and skeet shooting, polo, trout fishing, a herd of prize cattle, and

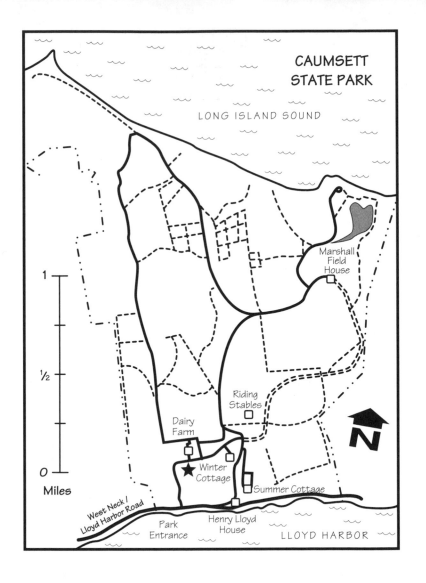

an extensive vegetable garden. None of the buildings is open to the public. They now house the Queens College Center for Environmental Teaching and Research, the BOCES Outdoor and Environmental Education Program, the Caumsett Equestrian Center, et cetera. For further information call 423–1770.

You will find here many specimen trees of interest—beech, oak, pine, dogwood, locust. You will find meadows, a salt marsh, and, below the large terrace of the main house, a pond where various waterfowl may be observed, and also the extensive shoreline along the sound. In the winter there is a good chance of seeing rare artic sea birds at the pond or along the shore.

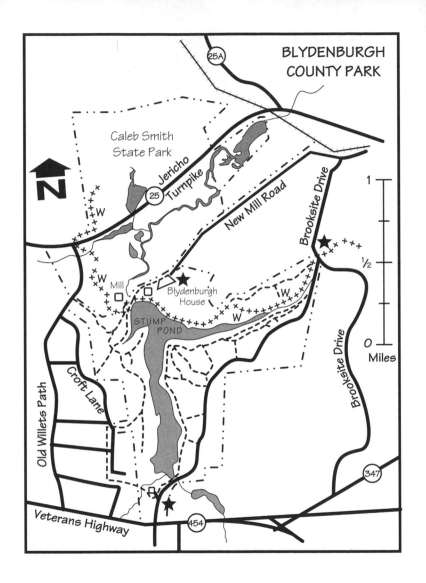

34

Blydenburgh County Park

East of Old Willets Path, this Suffolk County park has had a long history with very few owners. In 1798 Isaac Blydenburgh, seeing a good business opportunity, joined with some Smith relatives to buy the 588-acre parcel. They put in the dam that created the pond and erected grist, saw, and fulling mills, which flourished for a long time. Blydenburgh became the sole owner in 1801, erected the present house in 1821, and passed the property on to his heirs. In 1938 the property left the family to become David Weld's estate, and he in turn sold it to the county in 1968.

The park is mostly woodland with swamps and fields, and is home to Stump Pond, which we understand is second in size on Long Island only to Lake Ronkonkoma. The pond is long and irregularly shaped, somewhat like a boot with a pointed toe. No swimming is permitted, but rowboats are available, so it is a popular fishing place as well as campground. A number of trails and dirt roads make for easy walking; you'll also encounter horseback riders.

The park has two focal points for visitors. One is on the north side of Stump Pond, where the old homestead and mill are located, and the other is at the south end. Both have parking and limited visitor facilities, and they connect with each other by trails along both sides of the lake. The park is open dawn to dusk; the park office is near the south entrance (854–3713). The best way to reach the northern part is from the western edge of

Smithtown Branch on Route 25, Jericho Turnpike. Turn south off the turnpike at the traffic signal at Brooksite Drive and go one block, then west on New Mill Road, which leads directly into the park. The other part is reached from Veterans Highway (Route 454) just across from the road leading to the county buildings south of the highway.

Parking is limited in season to Suffolk County residents with permits. At other times of the year this restriction has not been rigorously enforced, and the chances are that the rangers will treat you with courtesy if you're not a nuisance.

Our suggestion for a good walk here is to follow the trail from the house by the north parking area down to Stump Pond. The trees near the house have all been planted but are native to the area. Once all this was tended farmland, but it was allowed some time ago to go back to nature. Now plants and surrounding shore are slowly filling in the lake, and it is all becoming overgrown. The area covered by the lake is 120 acres, and the fish consist of bass, sunfish, bluegills, as well as a few trout. The plants are common water lily and yellow pond lily, as well as water milfoil. You continue on the path southward across the dam by the mill and along the western shores of the lake to the stream, which you follow until the trail splits. Take the one to your left, which crosses the stream and goes up the hill, and then follow it back so that you reach the high bluff of the peninsula from which you see a whole panorama of the lake. The walk to this point is a little over a mile, and if you wish to extend it, you can continue along the fire road toward the southern reaches of the lake.

The trail soon turns away from the lake to come out on Croft Lane. Turn left here and continue on south, passing through a strip of woodland. Then go left just north of some county buildings, and downhill to cross a footbridge over the south inlet brook and on to a connection with the east shore trail at the park office. A complete circuit around Stump Pond is a good workout, since it is nearly 5 miles long, but it abounds with lovely views of the lake and its numerous waterfowl.

35

Bayard Cutting Arboretum and Heckscher State Park

Anyone familiar with New York's Central Park knows the genius of Frederick Law Olmsted in grouping trees together. See what he started here on the banks of the Connetquot River on a very rich man's estate in 1886. There are 690 acres with trim lawns and open meadows, a wildflower garden, a marshy refuge, and paths that lead everywhere. Along the river's edge, around and through woods, it is difficult to imagine a nicer walk anywhere or one with a setting more gracious than the one provided for public use here. The estate is maintained by the Long Island State Park and Recreation Commission, given in trust to the state by Mr. Cutting's daughter. There is no picnicking, but there is a $4.00 per car admission charge from early April to Labor Day and on weekends up to the last weekend in October. Hours are 10:00 A.M. to sunset Tuesday through Sunday (581–1002).

To reach the arboretum, take Southern State Parkway to Heckscher Parkway. Leave it at exit 45E and follow the signs east along Montauk Highway (Route 27A).

There are five different trails laid out and marked, each with different colors, and were you to take the allotted time on each, the total time suggested would be three and a half hours. We recommend that you plan to spend at least two and a half hours here and make a most pleasant morning or afternoon of it by

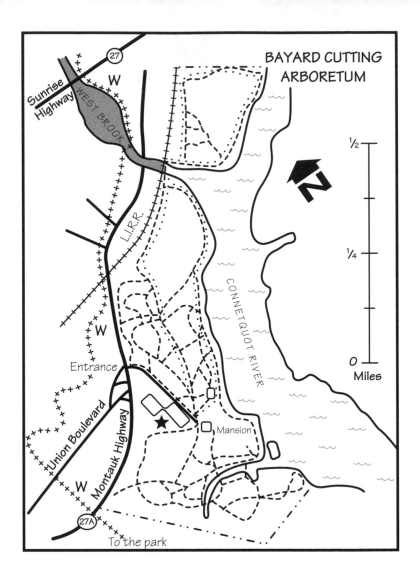

combining two or more of these walks into one longer one.

There is also a seasonal aspect to consider in planning your walk here. Wildflowers should be out in late March and April, rhododendrons in late May and June. Changing colors are engaging in October. Even on a hot summer's day, however, the welcome release is here; a cooling breeze off the river, shade from the mature trees, and benches conveniently at hand will probably quietly lure you to sit a spell.

The rambly, old, informal house is partially open. Tea and simple snacks are available in season, cafeteria style, and tables on the large, enclosed porch looking out over the river offer an attractive setting for a relaxing break.

Heckscher State Park has sandy beaches for swimming and a fine view of Great South Bay. It does, however, have a lot of wildlife in its interior. Naturally the deer, fox, pheasants, wild turkey, and other animals head for quiet areas in the populous peak of the day, but as sunset nears they get active again and more visible.

The Long Island Greenbelt Trail starts at the east end of parking field 8 on the edge of Great South Bay. (If field 8 is closed use the unnumbered field to the west of it. There is a concrete walkway connecting these two fields.) It can provide a pleasant shore, meadow, and woods walk for whatever distance time and energy permit. In fact, after about 4 miles it passes "just across the road" from the entrance to the arboretum.

Heckscher Park is heavily used in the summertime, but its nearly 1,700 acres can soak up a lot of people, and with the usual cool on-shore breeze from the bay, it can still be a lovely place. There are wildflowers in the wetlands and meadows in the spring, and in the fall monarch butterflies pass through in great numbers as they migrate south. The park is open daily from 8:00 A.M. to sunset and is reached simply by following the Heckscher Parkway extension of Southern State Parkway to the end. In the summer months there is a $5.00 charge per car, in the "shoulder" months (April, May, September, October) it's $4.00, and at other times free.

Marshes, Creeks, and Bogs

These aren't necessarily walks where you'll need your rubber footgear, but water figures prominently in each. It may be a lake or marsh that is full of birds to be observed, or it may be a brook or nascent river heading for the sea with a trail beside it that leads you through lush undergrowth or giant trees. In any case there will be a lot more visible life here than is common in the drier woodland walks. That of course carries with it the prospect of mosquitoes in season and muddy spots on the trails here and there. We've found these drawbacks unimportant compared to the larger pleasures of these walks.

These wetlands, and of course the ocean and sound beaches, reveal the great variety of natural beauty that has escaped the pressures of urban sprawl, the places where the ibis feeds in the salt marshes, where the beach plum covers the dunes with her spring blossoms, and the woodcock starts up from the cattails. These walks particularly call for you to bring along your binoculars and to proceed quietly along the paths.

Three of these walks are in very close proximity to "civilization," one being noisily close to Kennedy International Airport and the others only a few hundred feet from solid residential areas. That said, you'll find it easy to ignore the man-made noises and concentrate on the natural world. The birds and small animals are clearly undisturbed by their urban surroundings, and so can we be.

Another point to be made is that these walks may surprise you with the great numbers of waterfowl that now winter here, as compared to a few decades ago. Canada geese are especially common. At times it seems as though they have become permanent residents, not just visitors on their way south or north.

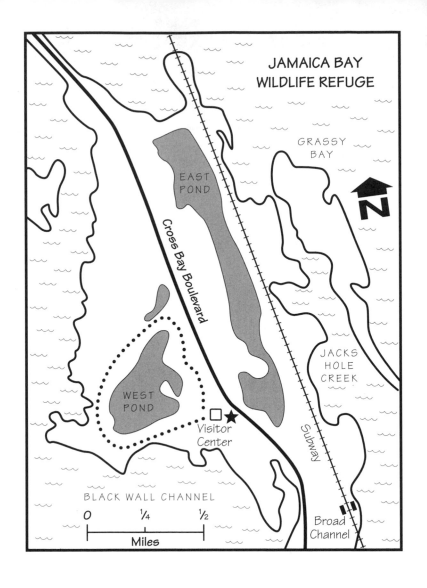

JAMAICA BAY
WILDLIFE REFUGE

GRASSY
BAY

EAST
POND

Cross Bay Boulevard

JACKS
HOLE
CREEK

Subway

WEST
POND

Visitor
Center

BLACK WALL CHANNEL

0   ¼   ½

Miles

Broad
Channel

36

Jamaica Bay Wildlife Refuge

The sun sets in a splash of color behind the towers of the city. A jumbo jet floats silently into Kennedy Airport on the other side of the bay. And West Pond at Jamaica Bay's Wildlife Refuge is alive, teeming with swooping terns, black skimmers seining their dinners through their amazing red bills, plovers and phalaropes skittering about in the shallows, the great egret and great blue heron standing, majestic in the tall reeds. This is late afternoon in early August. The juxtaposition here of what man hath wrought in the distance with the magnificence of nature in the foreground calls attention to the question of whether we can keep a balance between these sometimes inimical forces.

You need a permit to visit the refuge, but one is available (free) at the front desk of the visitor center, which is open daily 8:30 A.M. to 5:00 P.M. The refuge is now a part of Gateway National Recreation Area and hence the National Park system.

If you care to drive, take the Belt Parkway to exit 17S, then turn south on Cross Bay Boulevard. There is a parking lot at the visitor center; look for the one discreet sign. Or you can come by subway. The IND Far Rockaway A train takes you there (Broad Channel stop). In case you do, walk west from the station three short blocks through this residential area to Cross Bay Boulevard, then turn right and proceed ¾ mile to the refuge entrance.

The refuge itself comprises approximately 10,000 acres,

much of it islands and tidal marshes. The accessible spot is the West Pond region, and West Pond is a forty-five-acre brackish pond with a fine 1½-mile trail around it. A first trip to the Jamaica Bay Refuge is inspiring, especially undertaken at sunrise or sunset. Those responsible for seeing the possibilities, creating here a forever-wild area available to birds on the Atlantic flyway and people via the subway, deserve highest praise and homage. Sit on one of the benches and turn your glasses or scope on these creatures. Many will use Jamaica Bay as a regular stopover during spring or fall migrations. Maybe as you sit here, the short-eared owl will rise from the grasses and swoop about on his nocturnal search for a mouse or two. Even if you don't know one bird from another, the whole setting will impress you.

There are a few suggestions we'd make for enhancing your enjoyment here. Bring along your bird book and binoculars and, if it's a buggy time of year, your favorite insect repellent. Although there's usually a breeze and the bugs may not bother you, in some grassy protected areas, you may wish you had brought it along. Also, eat before you come. There are several picnic tables available outside the visitor center—which is the *only* area for picnicking, and there is no place to dine nearby. Remember too, please, that this is a nature refuge, not a park, so conduct that would disturb the wildlife (jogging, radios, pets, or cycling) is not permitted.

Across on the east side of the road, there is another, larger section of the refuge with a one-hundred-acre pond and shoreline on the bay as well. Sometimes rare birds stop here, and you may want to take a look, if you have strength after you walk around West Pond. If so, check first with the visitor center for trail conditions.

Please remember that all the vegetation makes a fine habitat for ticks and poison ivy, so take proper precautions against both.

The mailing address for information is Jamaica Bay Wildlife Refuge, Gateway NRA, Floyd Bennett Field, Brooklyn, NY 11234; (718) 318–4340.

37

John F. Kennedy Memorial Wildlife Sanctuary

As you fly into Kennedy Airport, you realize that the surrounding area is a vast network of tidal marshes, low-lying islands like lily pads in the bay, and barrier beaches conspicuously uninhabited by man, which causes us to speculate on wildlife there. Knowing that the sea rising over a marsh floods this land with chemical riches, that the ocean moderates temperatures here, and that wildlife in wetlands is abundant, we are intrigued by the thousands of acres behind Jones and Tobay Beaches. So if you speculate about this as we do, then we must recommend to you the John F. Kennedy Memorial Wildlife Sanctuary.

It is a 500-acre stretch, swallowed up by more than 5,000 acres owned by Oyster Bay Town and managed by the New York State Conservation Department, but it provides an opportunity to investigate something of what wetlands life is about. You must obtain a permit to visit the sanctuary either by mail (write to the Oyster Bay Department of Parks, Beach Division, 977 Hicksville Road, Massapequa, NY 11758 for an application), or by going to the office in person to get the permit on the spot. It is 1 block south of the Jerusalem Avenue intersection. Office hours are 9:00 A.M. to 4:30 P.M. daily; telephone number is 797–4110.

When you have your permit, get on the Ocean Parkway and go east about 4 miles from the Jones Beach traffic circle to the

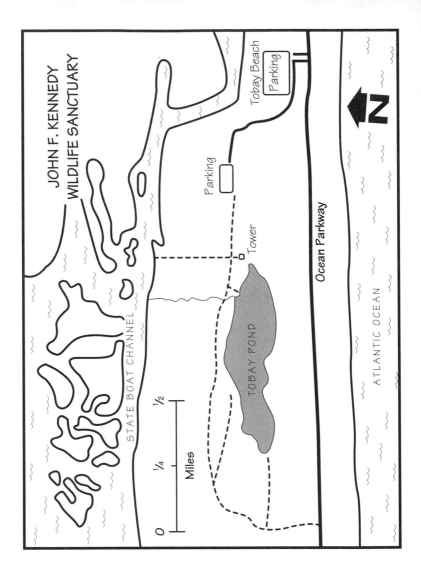

JOHN F. KENNEDY
WILDLIFE SANCTUARY

STATE BOAT CHANNEL

Tobay Beach
Parking

Parking

Tower

TOBAY POND

Ocean Parkway

ATLANTIC OCEAN

N

0   ¼   ½
Miles

Tobay Beach parking lot (just east of parking area 9). Drive west along the south border of the lot and along a road to the parking area provided for the sanctuary.

There is an old road, over a mile long, which leads through the middle of the area and provides good footing, although absolutely flat and unspectacular because it is bordered by plants growing to a height just over your head. You can leave the road in several places and walk to blinds or to the observation tower from which you can sweep your glasses over the pond and the treetops, but you cannot get much closer on foot to the water.

It was after Labor Day when we walked here, spent a longer time and walked farther than we intended, and were exhausted. From the tower we had watched a large brown female marsh hawk for some time, quartering low over the marshes, its white rump patch marking distinctly visible, its buoyant, tilting glide a joy to observe. There were clouds of tree swallows swooping about, and low cherry trees alive with cedar waxwings. We thought we saw a prothonotary warbler. Glossy ibis flew purposefully overhead. Duck arrived at the pond, skidding in for a landing. Kingbirds and white egrets were common, heron and belted kingfishers scarce.

The black-and-orange monarch butterflies were assembled in spectacular concentrations. These frail insects are noted for the long treks they make on their annual mass migrations and all morning continuously called attention to their flutterings.

Bayberry bushes were heavy with fruit; catbrier was in tangles. We noticed that birds had eaten the berries from the pokeweed. When we stretched out to rest on the white sandy dunes that overlook the pond from the northwest, we looked up at a sky everywhere interrupted by winged creatures.

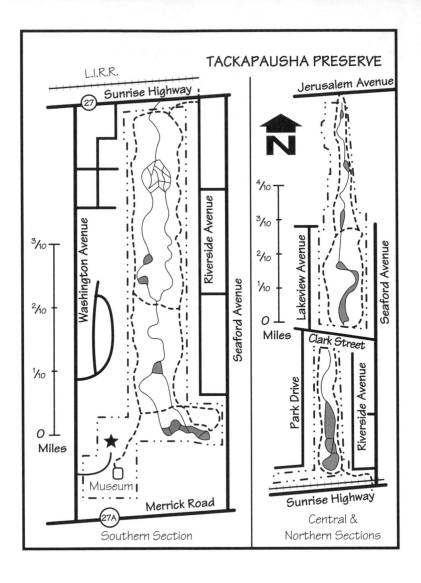

TACKAPAUSHA PRESERVE

L.I.R.R.

Sunrise Highway

27

Washington Avenue

Riverside Avenue

Seaford Avenue

³/₁₀

²/₁₀

¹/₁₀

0
Miles

★

Museum

Merrick Road

27A

Southern Section

Jerusalem Avenue

N

Lakeview Avenue

Seaford Avenue

⁴/₁₀

³/₁₀

²/₁₀

¹/₁₀

0
Miles

Clark Street

Park Drive

Riverside Avenue

Sunrise Highway

Central &
Northern Sections

38

Tackapausha Preserve

This surprising preserve encompasses eighty acres and a fine small museum in the middle of suburbia. A visit provides a pleasant contrast to the surrounding bustle and noise of this heavily developed area. The preserve is essentially a 1.5-mile-long and 1,000-foot-wide strip of woodland surrounding a fresh water stream (Seaford Creek) as it runs south toward the bay. It has three sections, separated by Clark Street and Sunrise Highway (Route 27), with the southern one, where the museum stands, starting just north of Merrick Road on Washington Avenue. Trails run along each side of the brook, so one can easily get up to a 3.5-mile loop walk if desired. Also, for the ambitious, there is a blazed link between these trails and the trails of Massapequa Preserve; it runs along the north side of Sunrise Highway.

Because the stream meanders and branches, there are lots of marshy areas and little ponds along the way, and to the sides there are taller trees. In the southern part you'll see white oak, red maple, and one of the very few remaining stands of Atlantic white cedar on Long Island. There are shadbush, spicebush, and highbush blueberry. On the ground you'll see fern, and in spring, flowers, such as wood anemone and pink lady's slipper.

Because of the variety of plants and insects, there are many different birds at any time of the year. A pamphlet listing nearly

200 species and times of year when you might expect to see them is available at the museum.

The central section comprises fifteen acres and a pond where mallards, green herons, and other water birds can be found. The northern section's forty-five acres is mostly a maple and oak forest, since it is higher and better drained, with wildflowers common in the open areas.

The museum building is a division of the Nassau County Museum of Natural History and well worth a visit. Inside there are informative displays, literature, and usually a nature film to see. Behind it there's a small menagerie with Long Island wildlife, allowing you a good close look at a red-tailed hawk, for instance. The museum is open Tuesday through Saturday 10:00 A.M. to 4:00 P.M., and Sunday 1:00 to 4:00 P.M., with a $1.00 admission fee for adults. The preserve, however, is open dawn to dusk. If you have questions, call 571–7443.

The name Tackapausha, incidentally, is preserved on the original deed for the land in Hempstead. Tackapausha was one of the sachems who agreed to the transfer of land to the early settlers. And that's all we know about him.

39

Massapequa Preserve

Like the Tackapausha Preserve, this has three sections: southern (Merrick Road to Sunrise Highway), central (to Clark Boulevard), and northern (to Linden Street). It is a quiet place in the midst of superhighways and dense population that offers a pleasant walk of a couple of miles up and back. A crystal-clear stream flowed freshly when we walked here; some kids fished at one of the dams, and two boys had a little rubber raft in the stream. The Massapequa Preserve is a wooded strip, drained by a stream dammed in a couple of places, thus making rather weedy ponds, excellent cover for ducks. The walking is either along a paved bicycle path that runs by the stream or along the Greenbelt-blazed foot trail, although there are paths into the woods and around ponds. In August the fragrance of sweet pepperbush permeated the air. We watched a least tern hover and dip over a pond, slamming into the water to capture a tiny minnow, and a family of black ducks float secretively through the reeds. Deep rose petals of the rose-mallow flowers, with their bright yellow centers, made a handsome display along the edge of the stream.

For an extended walk, park by Massapequa Lake at Merrick Road and follow the white-blazed Nassau-Suffolk Greenbelt Trail from its beginning there north to Sunrise Highway and on to Clark Boulevard. From there on in the northern part you'll have

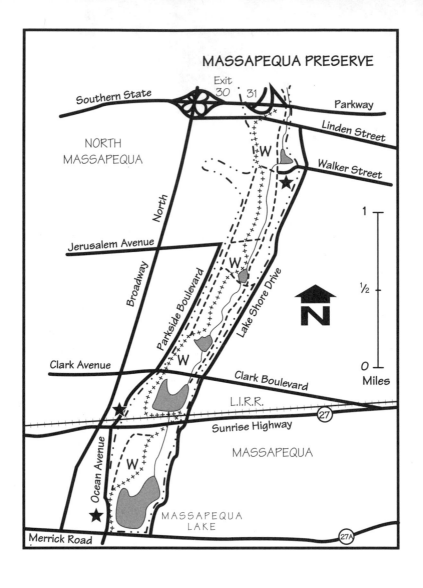

paved bicycle path on the east most of the way up to Linden Street. Parking is possible almost anywhere on Parkside Boulevard or Lake Shore Drive.

If you're really ambitious, you can follow the Greenbelt up to Bethpage State Park (about 6 miles) or all the way to Stillwell Woods and Cold Spring Harbor on the North Shore. The whole 22-mile stretch is best taken in easy stages!

In summer and in migration times, Massapequa Lake will usually have ospreys in evidence, and in winter a great variety of ducks (canvasback, coot, ruddy, etc.) will be at home. Other areas along the stream will reward you with whorled pogonia, white-fringed orchis, sundews, and more. The whole complex provides scarce habitat for many species and green space for people, making ecologists and nature enthusiasts rejoice. Similar areas can be found all along this south side of the glacial outwash plain.

Like Tackapausha, Massapequa Preserve is normally open dawn to dusk.

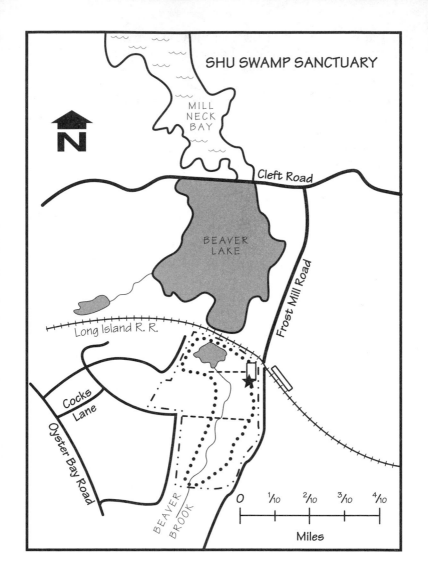

40

Shu Swamp Sanctuary

Shu Swamp Sanctuary is the jewel of the several properties owned and managed in the Mill Neck/Locust Valley area by the North Shore Wildlife Sanctuary, Inc. Tracing its origins back to 1929, Shu Swamp is a small but beautiful preserve featuring both wetlands and uplands, with most of the wildlife drawn there by the clear waters of Beaver Brook as it flows through. It's a lovely place to walk, passing on both sides of the marshy estuary that is filled with birds and magnificent trees.

One thing we must stress—wildlife preserves are not recreation areas, so that while visitors are welcome during daylight hours all year, they are asked to observe the posted rules, which forbid fires, camping, picnics, dogs, or any conduct not in keeping with the purposes for which these sanctuaries were established.

The sanctuary is open daily, except Friday, between 7:00 A.M. and 7:00 P.M. from April to October, and 7:00 A.M. to 5:00 P.M. from November through March. Note that the parking area is locked after hours, and parking along the road guarantees a ticket. A full-time warden, Mr. Thomas Hornosky, is in charge. The address is P.O. Box 214, Mill Neck, NY 11765; 671–0283. To reach the parking area, turn north off Route 25A on Wolver Hollow Road and follow it until it ends at Chicken Valley Road. Go right and continue 1.6 miles to Frost Mill Road. It leads right, bends left, and continues north to a viaduct over which the Long Island Rail Road tracks cross. The sanctuary parking area is just to the south of the tracks and west of Frost Mill Road.

We are prompted to write a few words about the tulip tree because the magnificent stand of tulip trees here along estuarial waters is inspiring, towering as they do probably 100 feet high, their trunks tall and straight and branchless for the first 50 or 60 feet. Considered the handsomest eastern forest tree because of its upright trunk and perfect symmetry, the tulip tree is frequently seen as an ornamental and is scattered throughout Long Island. However, the stand here is rare, perhaps unique, in number of trees well over 150 years old. Their old bark is rich brown and deeply fissured, and some must have diameters of 4 feet or more. Another name by which this tree is known is canoe tree, because the Native Americans made their dugouts from them, and when the English settlers first arrived they found the natives traveling all about Long Island in them. Surrounded by these ancient trees, looking up at those towering trunks, you may see how this was possible—though without modern tools it took great ingenuity and patience, skill with fire, and endless hours to fashion a seagoing craft of one. These trees give you reason to gasp and to consider the wonder of it all.

The North Shore Wildlife Sanctuary, Inc., is, like The Nature Conservancy, a private organization, grateful for your financial help, and contributions are tax deductible.

South Shore Nature Center

The South Shore Nature Center in East Islip is an interesting place to visit, for its 206 acres of woods and marsh give it a character rather different from most other South Shore preserves. In the first place, it is special because of the range of habitats it offers to wildlife—from a sandy shoreline on Great South Bay to marshes and then a dry upland forest. Secondly it has been so untouched by man that the 1¾ miles of trails are defined solely by dense underbrush in the woods and by plank walks in the wetter areas so that no blazes are needed. Indeed, the woods can be so dense that you can hear countless varieties of birds without seeing them.

The preserve is jointly owned by the Town of Islip, Suffolk County, and The Nature Conservancy, having been established in 1977 as a public recreation and outdoor education facility. The Town of Islip manages the area. All of the properties that make up the center were left in a natural state by their various owners well back into the previous century. As a consequence there is a great variety in the fauna and flora.

Most of the preserve's trees are red maple and black tupelo, which are found growing along the course of a stream and beside the boardwalks that span the preserve. An understory of sweet pepperbush, swamp azalea, and skunk cabbage flourishes in the freshwater bottomland along the stream, which flows through a

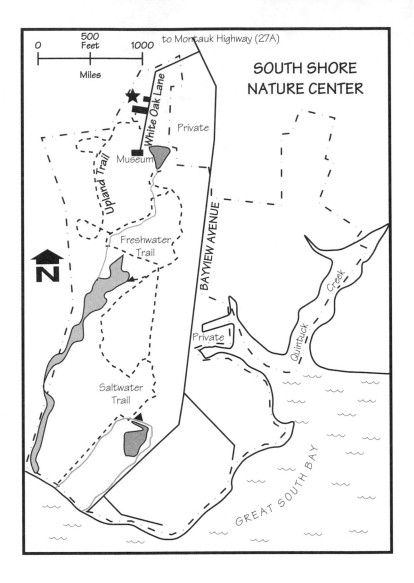

SOUTH SHORE
NATURE CENTER

to Montauk Highway (27A)

500 Feet
0   1000

Miles

White Oak Lane

Private

Museum

Upland Trail

Freshwater Trail

BAYVIEW AVENUE

Quintuck Creek

Private

Saltwater Trail

GREAT SOUTH BAY

N

small pond. Black cherry, white and black oak, mockernut hickory, and sassafras compete with the maple and tupelo in the preserve's drier northeastern part.

A large variety of woodland and aquatic birds visit the preserve in all seasons. Shorebirds such as sandpipers have also been seen in the fresh water areas as well as in the brackish region near salt water. Deer, small mammals, reptiles, and amphibians are also present—as are mosquitoes, since so much of the surface water barely moves through the marshy areas.

The trail system is most easily followed by taking the Upland Trail west and south from its start, close to the nature center museum building. The first quarter miles goes through terrain that is high enough to be above standing ground water, and as a result has a heavy growth of oak, mockernut hickory, and pitch pine. There are two side loops to the trail in this area that offer other glimpses of undisturbed habitat.

The first major trail junction on the left is marked to take you back to the nature center, and the one on the right is now the Freshwater Trail. Follow it and in a few minutes you'll come to another junction, with the Saltwater Trail on the right, leading down through marshy terrain toward Great South Bay. The left fork is the other route back.

The Saltwater Trail threads its way on elevated walkways through swamp and marshy areas overloaded with tall phragmites reeds, past a good-sized pond on the right, and down to a final junction. The left branch is your route back to the nature center, and the right one takes you a short distance to a viewing platform close to a large saltwater pond that directly connects with Great South Bay.

The preserve serves the local population well, not just by the museum and trails, but also through naturalists who are steadily engaged in teaching school and other groups about the trees and animals that make for a balanced ecological mix. It is open daily from 9:00 A.M. to 5:00 P.M from April through October (free admission). It is open weekdays only in the late fall and winter. For more information you can call 224–5436 or stop in the museum for informative pamphlets and a trail guide booklet.

To reach the preserve take Route 111 south from any of the major arteries (Long Island Expressway–Route 495, exit 56; Southern State Parkway, exit 43; Sunrise Highway–Route 27, Islip Avenue exit) to the end of Route 111 at the Montauk Highway (Route 27A). Go left (east) on it about 0.8 mile to Bayview Avenue. Turn right on Bayview; the preserve entrance will be on the right in about 0.8 mile.

Peconic River

South of Middle Country Road (Route 25) and west of Calverton is a large, sparsely populated area, mostly woodlands, with a series of ponds that form the stream that meanders to Riverhead, making the Peconic River the longest on Long Island. It is Robert Cushman Murphy County Park, a long, narrow strip of land on which Horn, Round, Peasys, Woodchoppers, Duck, Sandy, Grassy, Twin, and Jones Ponds follow one after another north to south. There are many sandy woods roads in this undeveloped area that make for pleasant walking, but there are so many such roads and trails that you need to pay close attention to your route so you don't get disoriented. The best map available is the one featuring the Long Island Pine Barrens Trail—West Section. (See the comments on this subject for Walk 23.) You can go safely any time of year, except during the winter hunting season. Call the New York State Department of Environmental Conservation at 444-0310 for the exact dates of the open season, and to get the required permit.

This area supports considerable wildlife. Deer are plentiful, and bird life abounds. We have seen at least twenty different mushroom species over the years. (Although we have rushed home afterward to look in our mushroom guide, we have never done more than photograph them.) The great blue heron lives in Woodchoppers Pond. You will see several species of duck, little

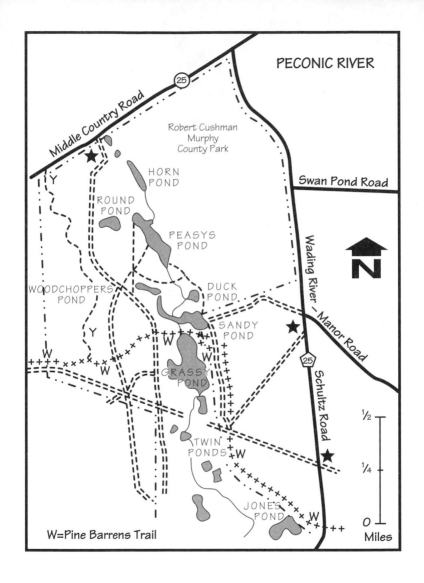

green heron, a Canada goose family, and, in the spring, warblers, orioles, scarlet tanagers, partridge, and woodcock. In summer, Kingbirds are often seen. We were thrilled to see the rare red crossbill among the pitch pine and oak. The shores of the ponds are marshy, and in the fall the colors are riotous. During rainy periods the trail can be wet in spots.

The half day or more you spend in this area will be peaceful—maybe a fisherman will be here, but we have met only one other hiker in the woods though we have walked here many times.

A good access to these boggy ponds is an unmarked road 2.3 miles north of Long Island Expressway exit 69 on Wading River/Schultz Road or 1.2 miles south on Wading River/Schultz Road from Route 25 and just opposite Wading River–Manor Road. It is a gated dirt road, with only informal provisions for parking on either side, near the posted signs reading COOPERATIVE HUNTING AREA. Another dirt road entry is on Middle Country Road, directly opposite a paved road named Panamoka Trail. Since the Pine Barrens Trail also cuts through this area, it could be used for access, starting at other road crossings.

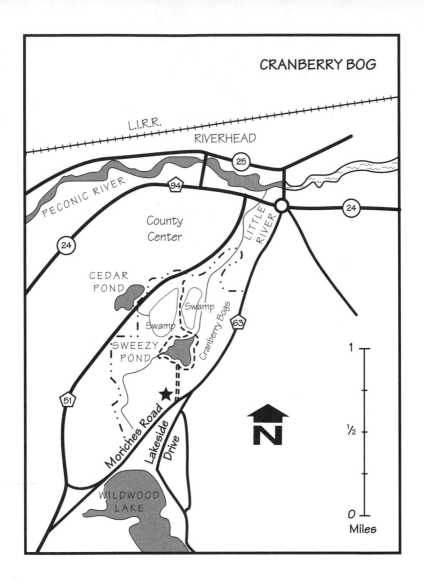

43

Cranberry Bog

A rather large area of county-owned land right in Riverhead is a 211-acre former cranberry bog. It is a unique haven for plant and animal life, probably the only remaining habitat of this type remaining on Long Island. Although it is unmarked, it is a favorite haunt of naturalists and has an interesting history.

In the early 1800s the Peconic River was in demand as a source of water power for mill wheels, but after the Civil War coal and other fuels took over, and the water was no longer needed as much. Someone had the sensible idea of using these lowlands and the abundant water for raising cranberries, and the resulting industry flourished from about 1875 to the 1930s, at one point becoming the third-largest producers of cranberries in the country. These small bogs could not compete with the major growers elsewhere, however; operating costs rose, and in 1959 a major pesticide used on cranberries gave the death blow by turning out to be carcinogenic.

This area is now held by Suffolk County as a preserve and nature-oriented park for its residents. An environmental staff oversees the preserve, but it is open for nature walks on an informal basis.

To find it, drive south on Route 63, which leads from Riverhead Circle toward Wildwood Lake. There are no signs, but there is a chain-link gate at the service road on your right, just after

Lakeside Drive, which veers off to the left. There is space to park a few cars.

Although the park gate is usually closed, there are a few unmarked trails, and you won't have any trouble walking around the gate. It is a place that makes a fascinating ramble. A bridge over the Little River makes it possible to make a loop around Sweezy Pond. The old cranberry fields lie to the east of the pond, and dikes permit you to penetrate some of the jungly growth. We say it is a ramble because to enjoy this spot is to explore, walking here and there along fringes of the wetlands. But we implore you: Walk quietly and cautiously, respecting stillness and wildlife. Deer and heron, swan and geese as well as duck, live here, so try especially hard not to disturb. The variety of shrub and ground cover is extraordinary—sweet pepperbush, bayberry, beach plum, wild grape, bearberry, cranberry, bear oak, so many bog plants—and the pond is full of water lilies, slender arrowhead, and reed, a catalog of freshwater swamplands growth. If you like this kind of exploring, you should enjoy a leisurely stroll here.

Incidentally, there is another series of old cranberry bogs nearby that are worth visiting. Referring to the Walk 42 map, take Wading River–Manor Road southeast from its junction with Schultz Road 1.1 miles to Old River Road (left). Proceed for about 1 mile on Old River Road to its junction with River Road. The bogs run both north and south from this point along a small stream that drains Swan Pond into the Peconic River. It's a pleasant area, often frequented by deer that come to drink from the stream.

Quogue Wildlife Refuge

The New York State Department of Environmental Conservation has had, since 1952, a long-term lease to manage this refuge, a 300-acre parcel that is the headwaters and drainage basin of the Quantuck Creek. This provides varied wetlands—swamp, freshwater bog, potholes, and ponds as well as tidal estuary. Also there are dwarf pine barrens up at the north end. Altogether there are 8 miles of trails, with the main ones noted on the map. The details of the way the place has been developed suggest talented and dedicated professional guidance. The sanctuary lies just north of the railroad tracks above the village of Quogue on Old Country Road, which runs north of the Montauk Highway and makes its way around into the Quogue–Riverhead Road (Route 104). The telephone number is 653–4771.

As you come into the preserve, there is a pen complex where animals are kept, most having been injured and unable to return to the wild. On our visit there was a bald eagle, bobcat, several wild turkeys, and other types of local animals. Ducks, geese, and other seasonal waterfowl roam at will at the pond's edge and use the adjacent area for foraging.

In spring Canada geese families go about training their young, parading in the grass, one parent ahead and one behind, and the little flock in between. Somehow they find the living so good here they stay year-round.

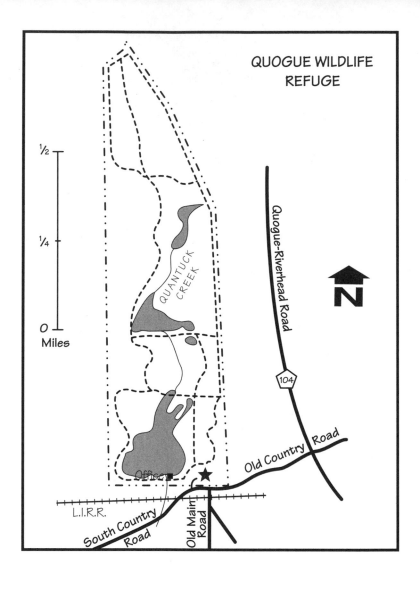

Walking is clear-cut. You can take the 0.7-mile path that goes around the main pond or the one that follows the perimeter of the refuge for more than 2 miles. We often decide to do both; a trail guide is available at the entrance booth.

Wherever you go you will see typical flora of the Long Island pine barrens—oak and pine interspersed with various berry bushes the birds like to feed on. The ground cover is bearberry and blueberry, and black cherry, beach plum, and shadbush, as well as nearly seventy varieties of wildflowers grow here. One summer we were delighted to find in a boggy spot a small stand of the exquisite, tiny, white-blossomed bog orchid; you also may find the insect-eating sundew and pitcher plants.

There are a number of places to sit and quietly observe, whichever path you take. Very often, on the ice pond on the north, there'll be a little green heron or some mallards. You can explore this refuge with no fear of getting lost. It is open daily from 9:00 A.M. to 5:00 P.M.

Sand Spits and Points

We've separated these walks from the sections devoted to Long Island's long, sandy shorelines, both north and south, mostly as a matter of convenience. These geographic features have the same water boundaries as the beaches and share the same varieties of vegetation and wildlife. Still, they are different in outlook, for most face land not very far off, most have calmer waters, and they just seem to have a different atmosphere.

One walk (Elizabeth A. Morton National Wildlife Refuge) is really practical only in the fall and winter, as ospreys, piping plovers, and colonies of terns nest there from April through August. The nesting areas are normally fenced off at that time to prevent people from disturbing these endangered birds.

The walks we've listed here all permit fairly extensive walking along the shoreline, though not as much as the beach walks. They remind us, though, that there are literally dozens of places where you can gain access to a calm shoreline, like these, in the off seasons. These are the town and county beaches that provide recreation along Great South Bay, the North Shore harbors, and the beaches along Peconic and Gardiners Bays. Other points of access are public roads that run right down to the water's edge. Usually there are parking restrictions, but off season and with local inquiry, you should be able to find many such places to walk.

Montauk Point, of course, is the one place that is fully exposed to the open Atlantic, and while it is often tranquil there, the steady erosion that is threatening the lighthouse tells of violent wave action at almost any time of the year. Also, in contrast to the other spots, Montauk has a quite extensive trail network inland from the beach that is worth exploring.

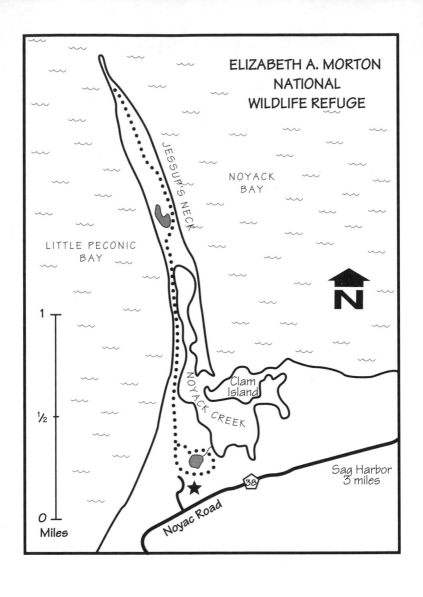

ELIZABETH A. MORTON
NATIONAL
WILDLIFE REFUGE

NOYACK
BAY

JESSUP'S NECK

LITTLE PECONIC
BAY

N

1

½

0
Miles

Clam
Island

NOYACK CREEK

Sag Harbor
3 miles

38

Noyac Road

Elizabeth A. Morton National Wildlife Refuge

Dividing Little Peconic Bay and Noyack Bay, jutting out from the north shore of the south fork of the island, just above Watermill, is Jessup's Neck. Of the numerous points, necks, and promontories that extend into the waters surrounding Long Island, this offers a wide variety of terrains, and walking here is great for many reasons. It is the Elizabeth Alexandra Morton National Wildlife Refuge and is managed by the U.S. Fish and Wildlife Service as a resting and feeding area for migratory birds. The refuge is open from sunrise till sunset.

Since the refuge offers a combination of beach, woods, ponds, and wetlands, walking is the ideal way for almost anyone to enjoy it, in any season and on any day. Entirely apart from the birding, the views over the waters are reason enough to visit.

The refuge is most easily reached by leaving Montauk Highway (Route 27) on Deerfield Road about 0.4 mile east of Water Mill, and heading north on it until you reach Noyac Road. Turn right on it and in about a half mile you'll reach the refuge. Drive into the grounds through a gate on the northern side of Noyac Road; park here near an old barn a few hundred yards beyond. Stop at the kiosk, which has a map and pictures, for a leaflet about the refuge.

While there is an office in the little building to the right beyond the parking area, it is rarely staffed, so any questions should normally be addressed to the Long Island National Wildlife Refuge Complex in Shirley (286–0485).

The path down to the bay is about a half mile and lined with many kinds of berry bushes—delectables for the land birds that frequent this quiet sanctuary. There is honeysuckle, myrtle, and rural charm. Be quiet and alert. We have come down this path on an early evening and surprised a graceful doe feasting on these same bushes. The path emerges upon a long, narrow strip of beach on the bay with a small inlet from Noyack Bay on the right. This area supports some 500 black ducks who winter here, as well as a variety of other water birds all year.

Now and then a clammer in the inlet leans out of his boat to scoop the bottom with his clamming rake. In fall or winter you'll see scallop boats in the bay dragging, though these juicy morsels are dwindling alarmingly, and nowhere else in the world does such a tiny, sweet, tender scallop exist.

The neck beyond this point is closed from April 1 to September 1, so as to leave the ospreys, piping plovers, and least terns that nest here quite undisturbed while they are raising their young. There is one active osprey nest near the far end of the inlet lagoon that you can easily see even in the closed season. As for the rest of the peninsula, plan on visiting it in fall and winter only. When you can walk there, in about a mile and a half you will come to a sharp rise and spread of land on a wooded promontory. We like to walk in the woods on the path and then return by the beach. At the beginning of the wooded path there was once a farmhouse. In the spring a carpet of daffodils appears out of the myrtle, splendid in color in this secluded habitat.

In the spring woods, during the warbler migration, you see some fifteen different varieties flitting among the big oaks before the leaves come out. And down on the beach to the west of the neck, look out to the fish weir where ospreys and cormorants often sit on poles where the pickings are concentrated.

The Morton Refuge can be a cool and refreshing place in

summer, when the afternoon breeze from the southwest whistles across the neck. In winter, when the bay freezes solid, if the winds across the ice are too chilling, there are many protected areas of woodland to the east before you reach the bay, and calm shelter for a walk under cover. One early spring we discovered a strangely eerie sight of dry white bones in a bed of greenest myrtle, the carcass of a deer dead of starvation or exhaustion. Later the refuge manager told us he had taken the skeleton to a school for preservation.

When you leave the parking area, you will quickly see a path leading right. This is a loop trail about 0.4 mile long that winds past a pond and through woods (devastated by Hurricane Bob in 1991) to rejoin the main trail about halfway to the beach.

Incidentally, this is one of more than 500 refuges managed by the U.S. Fish and Wildlife Service throughout the United States—many of them provide similar opportunities for walking and observing wildlife.

As with all other government parks, monuments, and refuges, there is a standard daily parking fee of $4.00 per private car or motorbike. Annual passes are also available for $10.00 for any one refuge, as well as several "Golden" passes for seniors or the disabled. For specifics, call the Fish and Wildlife Service at 286–0485.

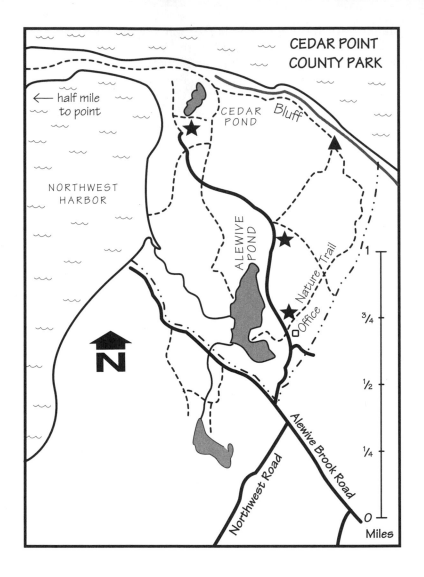

CEDAR POINT
COUNTY PARK

← half mile
to point

CEDAR
POND

Bluff

NORTHWEST
HARBOR

ALEWIVE
POND

Nature Trail

Office

N

Alewive Brook Road

Northwest Road

1

³/₄

¹/₂

¹/₄

0

Miles

46

Cedar Point County Park

In the town of East Hampton, 6.5 miles directly north of Georgica, occupying one of the many peninsulas that jut into Gardiner's Bay and give this area such meandering shapes, is Cedar Point, a choice park of 600 acres. This is a Suffolk County park, and you will find parking space here, as in all Suffolk County parks, limited to Suffolk County residents with permits. Trails are not heavy traffic areas, and hikers are not discouraged. For information, call 852–7620.

To find the park entrance if you're headed east on the Montauk Highway (Route 27), slow down as you pass the East Hampton Airport. The road signs were not made to be read while traveling 40 miles per hour. Turn north on the first road past the airport, Stephen Hands Path. Continue on it 2 miles, across Route 114; it connects with Old Northwest Road, which bears off to the left. Continue on this for 1.8 miles to a fork, where you go right on Northwest Road, 1.7 miles to the crossing with Alewive Brook Road. Jog left and enter the park there to the north. Or, driving from East Hampton, follow Three Mile Harbor Road and turn left on Springy Banks Road, which also runs into Alewive Brook Road.

You enter the Northwest Woods, a high bluff generally 50 feet above the waters of Gardiners Bay to the north, and drop down alongside Alewive Pond to Cedar Pond, near which you'll find a camping and parking area. There are deer in these woods; look sharply in the late afternoon. When you park, you can walk out on the spit, which points west. It's a fine walk, with a striking granite lighthouse at the tip. And though surely you may temporarily lose your sense of direction, you'll look south onto Northwest Harbor and Barcelona Point, northwest onto Shelter Island, north onto Orient Beach State Park, and east onto Gardiners Island; eventually the geography of these fingers and watery shores will sort itself out.

There's a good nature trail (leaflets available) running from the park office area opposite Alewive Pond, 0.7 mile out to an observation platform at the top of the bluffs overlooking Gardiners Bay. On a clear day you should easily see the Connecticut shore 15 miles away beyond Orient Point.

The walk west to Cedar Point is just over a mile. The inner shore is sandy, the outer one pebbly. From this entry east along a stretch of wild beaches to Lafarges Landing is a distance of 2 miles. Whichever way you choose to go will be delightful, particularly in early spring or fall—summer afternoons can be crowded. Jingle shells, scallop shells, boat shells, or slipper shells and pear-shaped whelks are nature's handiworks you'll find here, along with all the other flotsam that give beachcombing variety. Between the open woods and the sand spit there is a lot of fine habitat for birds.

The park is open all year, basically from 8:00 A.M. to dusk. That means the gates close about 4:00 P.M. from November through February.

Orient Beach State Park

At the end of Route 25 on the north fork of Long Island, just before you get to the water and the ferry to New London, on your right is the usual rustic state park sign for Orient Beach—but Orient Beach is not a usual state park. Turn and drive along the causeway to the parking lot. If it's spring or early summer, look to your right as you go along the causeway for the osprey nest across the water. A faithful pair returns yearly, and they are magnificent birds, these fish hawks. Sometimes you can watch them fish, diving from on high and catching a fish as much as 10 feet below the surface with their talons.

The park (323–2440) is open daily all year, 8:00 A.M. to 4:30 P.M. October through May, 8:00 A.M. to 6:00 P.M. in June and September, and 8:00 A.M. to 8:00 P.M. in July and August. The parking fee is $5.00 in June, July, and August. After 4:00 P.M. there is never a charge. The summer months are the most crowded time and not one we particularly recommend because when you walk from the parking lot out onto the beach and turn to your right, you'll find it is a favorite picnicking and swimming spot. One hundred yards past the lifeguard, however, you escape the bulk of the crowd. As you move around the curve of the beach, you have the choice of keeping to the edge of the water or following the jeep tracks into the interior of this spit. You may be confused because Orient Point looks to the northeast, but this

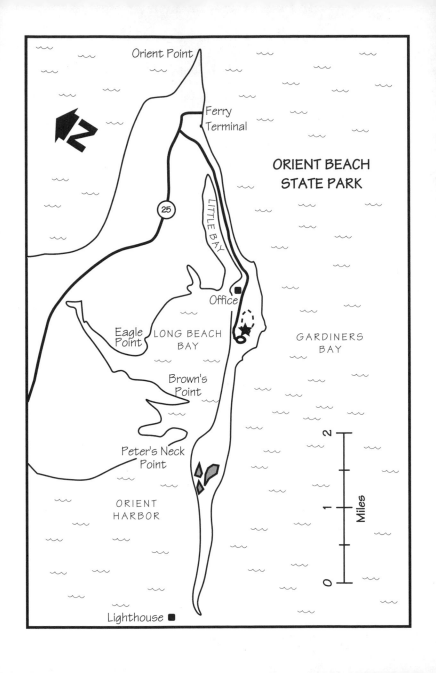

narrow strip of land that is Orient Beach, 4 miles long, runs to the southwest.

What makes it unusual? It affords beautiful views of Gardiners Bay and its shores and islands. Wander at will among the scrub pine, for you are never far from salt water on either side. There are two ponds in the interior that attract water birds, and here among the stunted pines and wetlands there is a herd of deer that comes and goes to the mainland. Although we have seen their tracks many times, we have actually seen the deer only fleetingly in winter. You cannot be quiet enough to surprise these wily, graceful creatures, but how they can conceal themselves in this narrow quarter is a mystery. They blend in and get lost as nature intended.

A good plan is to go out by the beach, pebbly but not bad footing, and back through the interior. If you get as far as the tip, you will come near the handsomely rebuilt Long Beach Bar Light (locally called the "Bug" Light), whose predecessors guided fishing boats into Greenport. Be prepared, though, to find this farthest end closed to visitors in spring and summer, since then it is home to a nesting colony of piping plovers.

Incidentally, now that you've come this far east, you ought to continue a couple of blocks farther north to the parking area at the absolute end of Route 25, just beyond the New London ferry terminal. If you leave your car there and walk along the beach about a half mile to the bitter end, you'll enjoy a panorama of Long Island Sound and the Connecticut shore, Block Island Sound, Montauk Point, Gardiners Island, and Gardiners Bay. Directly across the tide rips of Plum Gut is Plum Island, a closed area that is home to the U.S. Department of Agriculture's Animal Disease Center.

You should also make the time to walk the new Latham Maritime Forest Trail, a nice nature trail that starts out at the north end of the parking lot, meanders up the spit and down again to the parking area. It's well laid out and has a very relevant leaflet for the dozen stations along it.

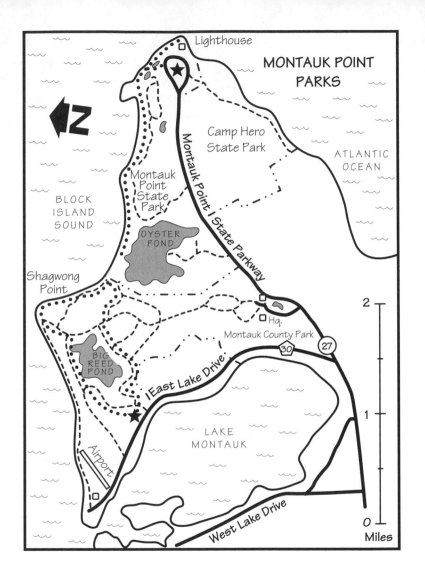

48

Montauk Point Parks

This is an extremely popular area, and the crowds may put you off, but don't let them—you'd be missing too much if you did. Choose your time and move away from crowds. Montauk is an experience, and you are apt to enjoy it if you are a loner and nature lover. There's a raw bleakness here: hills of shadbush and bayberry, almost endless dunes, and an incessant surf chewing away at the boulders, tumbling stones that cackle in a noisy babble. We've come here at dawn before the sun was up at least twice and will come again. If you come at this hour, you won't be alone. Surf fishermen will be here before you. You can walk for miles in either direction. We've been here at midday and at sunset, too, lingering afterward in the twilight. So, although it is wiser to rhapsodize about winter, spring, or fall, our experience is that there's something for you in any season at any hour of day in Montauk.

The public lands east of Lake Montauk are quite extensive, as they include the 724-acre state park that extends west from the point about 2 miles to encompass the northern shoreline and Oyster Pond. Directly west of it is Suffolk County's "Theodore Roosevelt County Park," whose 1,200 acres cover Shagwong Point and most of the remaining land east of East Lake Drive (excluding a residential area at the middle section of that road). The next property is the undeveloped 700-acre Camp

Hero State Park. It is located south of the highway and away from the lighthouse and formerly was the site of an Air Force radar station. Although it is not easily accessible, the bluffs are impressive when viewed from the beach. Finally, west of Camp Hero is a new 330-acre nature sanctuary.

The present county park headquarters building, called the Third House, dates in part to 1806, when it was erected for those tending cattle on the surrounding 10,000-acre common pasture. Since then it has served as a residence for Theodore Roosevelt and his Rough Riders after the Spanish-American War, and in the 1930s it became the Deep Hollow Guest and Cattle Ranch. Today the only remaining horsey aspect is a riding stable. The hilly terrain here offers good protection from bad weather, and as a result many varieties of birds and animals inhabit the area.

Where to go at the point? Start by visiting the lighthouse and the fine small museum there that will give you a better understanding of the continuing conflict between sea and man here. Ocean storms erode the point and endanger the lighthouse; man moves in boulders at the base of the bluffs to lessen erosion, and is attempting, successfully we're told, to cover the steep slope with vegetation that holds the soil in place.

Then, follow the path north of the lighthouse down into the gully to the little pond. Wildflowers, birds of the thicket, and pond life are here. Then cross over the dunes on to the beach and walk south to the point. If you're here at low tide, you can walk as far south and west along the rocky shore as you are able. The other direction—northwest along the beach fronting Block Island Sound—is a less crowded walk; the farther you go, the fewer the people and the more abundant the shorebirds. Montauk is a prime birding area, especially for artic seabirds.

These parks cover a large area, so if you walk only those beaches easily accessible from the main parking area, you have not done justice in exploring the region. If you drive north off the highway on East Lake Drive, stop to sample the county park nature trail, and continue on beyond the lake and the airport to your right to one of the parking places at the very end of the road. From here you can walk eastward on the shore toward Shagwong Point and beyond.

A map of the Montauk area with the various trails is available at the county park headquarters on Route 27. A somewhat dated but more complete map is available from the town of East Hampton; refer to Walk 27 for the address.

If you have questions, call 668–5000 for the state park, and 852–7878 for the Suffolk County park. Both are open daily from 8:00 A.M. to 5:00 P.M.

North Shore Beaches and Bluffs

While similar in extent to the marvelous strands of the South Shore, these beaches are quite different in character. They tend in general to be more pebbly, since the sea is constantly eroding, not a long sandbar, but the back side of a glacial moraine. As a result the beaches have lots of stones, from golf-ball-sized up to impressive glacial erratics, so sandy spots for swimming and sunning are somewhat scarce. The stones, in turn, have been mined from a nearly continuous line of bluffs that mark the coast. These can be well over 100 feet high, as at Mt. Sinai, and they are usually wooded up to the edge except where homes have been built. Both these factors often make beach access difficult even while providing fine views out over Long Island Sound. In many places the bluffs are so high and steep that the only way homeowners can get down to the water's edge is by erecting long wooden stairways down the face. The bluffs look most impressive when seen from a boat offshore; they must be intimidating close up!

There are a few places in the long stretch east of Port Jefferson where the bluffs are minimal. Most of these spots have either a public or private road down to the beach, for swimmers in the summer and surf fishermen at any time. In general we've usually encountered fewer people on these North Shore beaches than on the south. The parking situation noted for the Atlantic beaches, however, can also apply here.

One other factor that sets these shores apart is the tidal range. On the South Shore the range is only about 3 feet, and between high and low tides the look of the sandy strand changes very little. On the North Shore the range varies from about 4 feet at Horton Point to over 7 feet at Glen Cove. This makes for a markedly different seashore, due to the exposed rocky intertidal zone.

Wildwood State Park

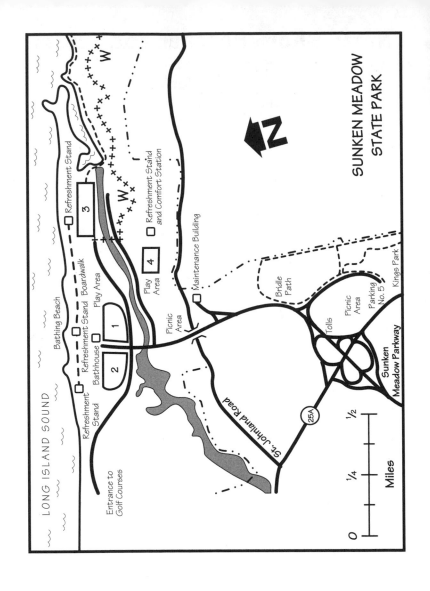

SUNKEN MEADOW
STATE PARK

49

Sunken Meadow State Park

Sunken Meadow State Park is a grand place for walking, most particularly when it's not swimming weather. Take a nice, crisp fall weekend to go or a soft spring day or even a misty summer's day, for there are miles to explore. An interesting inlet lies to the east, a bridle path to the south, the beach itself as far west as you could wish, and in the middle of it all a fine ¾-mile boardwalk.

This beautiful park, which has one of the best sand beaches on the North Shore, was opened to the public back in the 1920s when the legendary Robert Moses acquired an abandoned estate here. He saw its possibilities for a public recreation area on the sound directly north of the state park that bears his name on the South Shore. Now there are four large parking lots, three golf courses, picnic areas and playgrounds, and refreshment stands. Sunken Meadow is a highly organized place, well adapted to lots of visitors, but it all quiets down in the off season.

The walk we enjoy the most is to take the Greenbelt Trail east, from its beginning at the footbridge close to the southwest end of parking field 3, along the high bluffs to Old Dock Road. There you can drop down to beach level and return along the shore until you can cross over again to lot 3. This 2.5-mile loop gives you fine views of the Nissequogue inlet and estuary, salt meadows, and a long stretch of beach extending in both directions. If field 3 is closed, park in field 1 and walk east to the bridge.

As you might expect, the 200 acres of sandy bluffs, brackish creeks, salt marshes, and heavily wooded uplands offer excellent habitat for birds in all seasons. Eighty-four varieties are common in one season or another, and sixty more are occasionally seen here, so bring your binoculars.

Stop at the park office in the building between the west end of field 1 and the sound, and get a free checklist and guide covering the 121 varieties that have been observed more than once in five years. It also shows the seasonal abundance for all these types of birds.

The park is open 6:30 A.M. to sunset in the summer season. The toll is now $5.00, and it is levied weekdays from 7:00 A.M. to 4:00 P.M. and on weekends from 7:00 A.M. to 6:00 P.M. in the summer. The toll is collected on weekends from 8:00 A.M. to 4:00 P.M. in May and September; at all other times the park is free (including summer weekdays for seniors). Questions? Call 269–4333.

The best roads to take to reach the park are major arteries such as the Long Island Expressway (Route 495), Jericho Turnpike (Route 25), Northern State Parkway, and Route 25A. All of them intersect with and give easy access to the sole entrance road, the Sunken Meadow Parkway.

50

Nissequogue Estuary

A blazed trail, the Long Island Greenbelt, winds across the full width of Long Island and has since 1978, going northward 32 miles from Great South Bay to Long Island Sound. This was made possible through the inspiration and initiative of the Long Island Greenbelt Trail Conference, combined with the cooperative effort of the Towns of Islip and Smithtown, Suffolk County and New York State. It is a noteworthy accomplishment.

Anyone may walk the trail, which has locked gates where it enters nature preserves, but you must have a permit to get the lock combinations (call 265–1054, Caleb Smith State Park). The conference prints a map of the Long Island Greenbelt that shows this part of the trail in much more detail than our map. It is otainable for $2.00 through the Long Island Greenbelt Trail Conference, Inc., 23 Deer Path Road, Central Islip, NY 11722; 360–0753.

After leaving Blydenburgh County Park and Caleb Smith State Park, both of which have walks (34 and 21) that can conveniently be done from a central location, the Greenbelt Trail heads north toward its end at Sunken Meadow State Park. This section is a linear one, with more road walking than is desirable, so we can't really recommend the first part of it.

Most of the last 4½ miles, however, are so rewarding that we urge you to find a friend and spot cars at each end so you can cover it more easily. The trail basically follows the south shore of

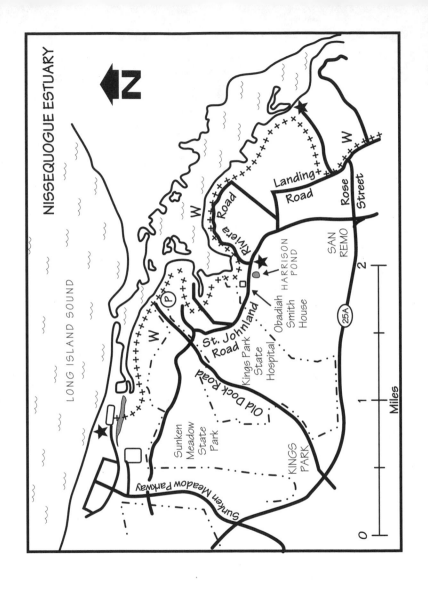

NISSEQUOGUE ESTUARY

LONG ISLAND SOUND

Sunken Meadow State Park

Sunken Meadow Parkway

Old Dock Road

St. Johnland Road

Kings Park State Hospital

Obadiah Smith House

HARRISON POND

Riviera Road

Landing Road

Rose Street

SAN REMO

KINGS PARK

25A

0   1   2   Miles

the Nissequogue River, sometimes close to the water, sometimes well above it on bluffs.

To start at the south end of this lovely stretch, find the corner where Route 25A makes a right-angle turn in San Remo, about 1.7 miles north of the junction with Route 25 in Smithtown. At the corner go straight east on Rose Street for about 0.4 mile until it ends at Landing Avenue. Turn left there, and in 0.2 mile turn right into the long downhill driveway of the Smithtown Landing Club Town Park. Go down to the end, park there amid the golfers, and find the Greenbelt blazes. They are vertical white blazes about 2 inches by 4 inches painted on trees, rocks, and posts and should be easy to pick up here. The trail heads north along the shoreline again, reaches Riviera Road, and continues on it along the curve of the river. When you reach St. Johnland Road, the trail goes right for a short distance. Right across the street the parking area for the Harrison Pond Town Park is an alternate place to leave a car.

Just below the Obadiah Smith House, the trail leaves the road and cuts north across the marsh. Go in here at the double blaze. Remember that a single blaze means you're still on the right track; a double one signals a change in direction.

The path crosses through tall reeds, follows along the river, climbs a bluff for a fine view, and continues on to Old Dock Road. You'll find a restaurant and boating facilities and another place you can park off season.

When you take the trail up the 150-foot bluff to the west, you enter Sunken Meadow State Park and can now follow the route along the top until you come down into the developed part of the park. There the trail makes a sharp turn across a footbridge to end just across the road from parking lot 3.

From this last stretch of bluffs, you can see where the river reaches the sound; beyond it is Short Beach, which belongs to the village of Nissequogue, and Crane Neck Point across Smithtown Bay. Across the sound is Connecticut, of course, and the city with the tall buildings is Bridgeport. There are always boats of many sizes, which move in a businesslike way across the sound's waters and, in the river, swans, which have a close affinity to Long Island. This section of the trail provides picture-postcard views all along the bluffs, and when the waterfowl migrate, it can be spectacular. The bluffs are popular, so for the quiet moods that the trail does have, it is best to walk here early in the morning—or late on a summer's day to watch the sunset.

51

Wildwood State Park

Wildwood State Park is well out on the island, 73 miles east of New York City. It is roughly rectangular and has a frontage of about 1.5 miles on Long Island Sound. Situated on high ground with high bluffs, it covers just over 700 acres. There is good walking along the pebbly North Shore beach here. Also, within the park, there are about 10 miles of trails through cleared woodland areas, offering easy walking straightaways that are fairly level, nothing strenuous. It is a place that is open, protected, quiet, and wooded. And you can walk at a good clip.

Many of the North Shore beaches are private, not allowing easy access without trespassing, but there is a large parking lot here with a broad walkway leading down a gradual slope, less than a quarter mile to the beach. The sand doesn't shift along these North Shore beaches as rapidly as it does along the Atlantic. The water freezes up much more quickly and warms earlier in the spring. The ground is gravelly, and there are quite a few boulders, debris of the glacial period. Protected as the beach is by these high bluffs, it is a marked contrast to the ocean shore and offers good variety to a beach walker. There's less severe buffeting in windy weather, too. Those close relatives of the crab—barnacles—have attached themselves to all boulders. Seaweed in many forms is exposed. Periwinkles and whelks abound. The narrow strip of this tidal zone teems with life, hidden be-

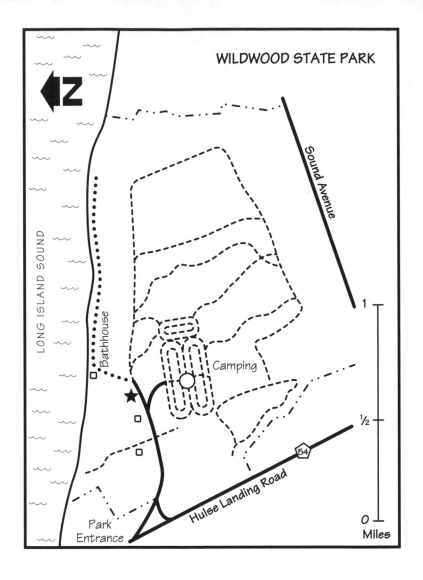

tween rocks and usually ignored by all except the most curious persons. Wildwood State Park, however, does have a considerable population because of a large tent-camping area and trailer camp, so it is a popular weekend retreat and a bit too crowded during the summer if you seek a lonely stretch. Plan to walk in Wildwood out of season, when it will be rewarding. It's open all year, dawn to dusk.

To get to Wildwood, take Route 54, Hulse Landing Road, north from Route 25A. It is just east of Wading River (929–4314).

Quite naturally the inland trails are places less frequented, although they are more protected and easier walking than the beach. If it weren't for the trees along the North Shore, erosion would have taken most of Long Island into the sound. So walk here to discover the woodland, the home of numerous insects, birds, and mammals, and bring along a curiosity to get to know still another tree, shrub, or creature with whom we share the earth.

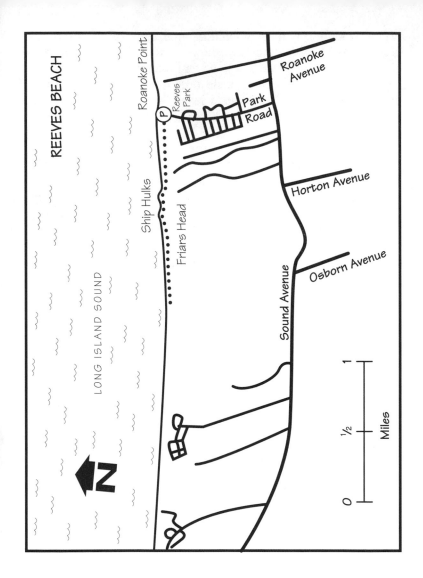

52

Reeves Beach

The town of Riverhead maintains a beach at the end of Roanoke Avenue on Long Island Sound. Off season, there is usually no problem parking, though during summer months a permit is required (obtainable at the town recreation department). The bluffs on the sound are extremely high, the beach at the tide line quite pebbly with some impressive glacial erratics, and, just west a half mile, strewn with two ship hulks, wrecks of some time past. It's a steep walk down to the beach from the parking spot. Turn left and walk a couple of hundred yards, and you will be alone.

For miles along here the border of high wooded bluffs obscures any houses, and there is a feeling of immense loneliness. There are especially wide areas and big tangles of the purple beach pea, sea rocket, and bishop's weed. Some reeds at the base of the bluffs are so tall you can be completely concealed by them. It is nice exploring territory. Tangles of growth conceal old driftwood, and there are wild beach flowers. Fishing offshore here must be pretty good; there are frequently clusters of small boats bobbing not far out and an occasional surfcaster.

We have walked this beach many times, but never during swimming season. Its setting—the beach is tucked down under a high ridge—appeals to us. In a winter rain the Connecticut shoreline is completely obscured. With snow on the frozen ground, you cover distances faster. In early spring we find trailing arbutus on paths up the bluffs, with wintergreen and partridge berry. The trailing arbutus is particularly satisfying to come upon in blossom, such a delicate fragrance and the tiny, palest lavender petals. On fresh, bright sunny weekends, the promise of a good breeze brings many sails out on the sound, and the clarity lets you see details on the opposite shores. Falling autumn leaves pile up in the gullies, cover paths, and rustle when you pass along. Because we never have any particular objective in mind, we always look at a watch as we start off headed west, and when we remember to look again, we are always surprised by the lateness of the hour. We usually take along field glasses and a camera.

How to get there? Follow Roanoke Avenue north from the Route 58 traffic circle in Riverhead until it ends at Sound Avenue. Then turn left, west, and go a short distance to the second road, Park Road. Turn right, north, and follow up and down a hill or two. The road ends in a modest parking area that overlooks Reeves Beach.

53

Horton Point Park

The Horton Point Lighthouse sits serenely, looking something like a canvas by Edward Hopper, high over the waters of Long Island Sound facing Connecticut. It is the chief ornament of a tree-shaded Town of Southold park, which is a beautiful place to picnic. The broad view from this high bluff allegedly led George Washington to recommend a light here when he passed through in 1757 on his way to Boston. That's a bit of oral history, but the construction in 1857 of the first of a series of more modern lights here is well documented. Today the keeper's house contains an excellent, small marine museum which, like the lighthouse, has been sponsored and improved by the Southold Historical Society.

The eight-acre park provides one of the best seascapes on Long Island's North Shore. Here one can view the sound and visualize its many moods, its past and present commerce and the challenges that faced Long Island refugees traveling to and from the Connecticut coast when Eastern Long Island was occupied by the British from 1777 to 1784.

One hundred thirty-two wooden steps take you down to the boulder-strewn beach. In all kinds of weather it is picturesque because of fisher-folk. They take blackfish from around those rocks. They dig their poles into the sand, light their pipes, and keep an eye on the floats, ready to jump and reel in when they bob. We always check to see if they have a few in their pails.

Walking on Horton's beach can be rough because of the peb-

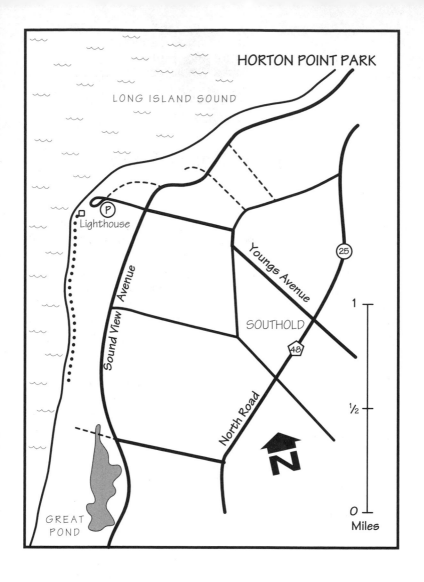

bles, but good for massaging the insteps. Snorkeling is popular here. It's one of the few places on Long Island where we see people in wet suits with scuba tanks and flippers. The huge rocks are relics of the Ice Age.

There is a long beach stretch here to the west that seems uninhabited, very wide with lots of driftwood. And the flotsam that heaves itself up on the beach is fascinating.

Standing on these North Shore bluffs makes Long Island's formation in the geological past become fundamentally clear. You can imagine the great pushing blade of the glaciers, for geologists say Long Island is wholly the result of the glaciers, shoving a wide, wide swath of sand, soil, rock, and tops of mountains southward like a massive bulldozer and piling it here. Then the ice melted and the waters ran off, washing the soils southward into a plain. The colossal scale of the whole thing can be appreciated when you realize that the ocean was raised to its present level, more than 300 feet higher than it had been, by the melted ice to form Long Island Sound. And what capriciousness there was in shoving and raising the level of the waters can be seen in the structure of peninsulas and spits and tiny islands that make up the shape of the map today.

The force that could bring these huge boulders can be better appreciated when you walk along the beach here, comparing your size to their size. Surely the experience is a universal one, and it is one that will linger with you.

The museum alone is worth a visit if you have any interest in matters nautical or, indeed, local. The collection of scrimshaw, tools, maps, letters, ships' logs and journals, paintings, and more is splendid. You can also climb the tower to inspect the working light and enjoy the view. The museum is normally open on weekends from 11:30 A.M. to 4:00 P.M., between Memorial Day and Columbus Day, but it would be well to check with the historical society in Southold before your visit (765–5500), as special visits can be arranged at other times.

A word on getting here. Take the Route 25/48 divided highway (North Road) east from Mattituck until you come to the turnoff for Southold Village (Youngs Avenue). Instead of going right, turn left on Youngs and follow it, past the jog at Sound View Avenue, to the very end.

About the Authors

"We are not hikers—we aren't that goal-oriented." So say the Albrights, trying to make the distinction between walking to get somewhere and walking for fun. For them walking is to look and listen to all the sights and sounds of the woods, the meadows, and the sea.

Priscilla and Rod Albright lived in New York most of their adult lives; having come East to college, they stayed right on. Rod was a television producer for a large advertising agency, and Priscilla served on the boards of several social services agencies.

Now retired, they do their daily walks from three different bases: in summer on an island in the Bay of Fundy where the craggy shores offer some scrambling and the woodland paths are full of birds and blueberries; in fall and spring they walk in the foothills of the White Mountains from a cottage in South Parsonsfield, Maine, near the New Hampshire border; come the depths of winter, a small Airstream trailer goes with them to Florida and Florida trails on pine needles or to the Southwest to walk in canyons or the floor of deserts because they are insatiably curious about the natural world.

Robert L. Wendt, who also updated and revised the fourth and fifth editions, has been an active walker and outdoorsman in the New York area for many years. Active in the Appalachian Mountain Club and in mapping Long Island trails, he brings broad experience in the field to this task.

Notes

Notes

Notes

Notes

Try other **Short Nature Walks** books!

Short Nature Walks in Connecticut   *$10.95*
Fifty walks are outlined in this much-loved guide!
Nearly 500 miles of maintained trails to cover.

Short Nature Walks on Cape Cod,
Nantucket, and the Vineyard   *$10.95*
Explore the natural beauty of Cape Cod and the
Islands in all their fascinating variety.

Looking for some **biking** tours? Try this guide:

Short Bike Rides on Long Island   *$12.95*
Take your time and pedal at a comfortable pace
past grand estates and vast farm fields.